RECONSTRUCTING THE REAL YOU

APPLYING ASTROLOGY TO FAMILY PSYCHOLOGY

BARRY D. COWGER
WITH MARTHA M. CHRISTY

FOREWORD BY
JEFFREY GREEN

D1528920

Mercurius Publishing
Box 156, Scottsdale, Arizona 85252
602-949-6007 * Fax 602-991-8387

RECONSTRUCTING THE REAL YOU
APPLYING ASTROLOGY
TO FAMILY PSYCHOLOGY

BY BARRY D. COWGER
with Martha Christy

Foreword by Jeffrey Green

This book is manufactured in the United States of America. First edition.

ISBN: 0-9632091-1-6

DISCLAIMER
No part of the material presented in this book is intended to supersede or replace the services, advice or opinions of professional psychiatrists, psychologists, counselors or health care practitioners.

Single copies may be ordered directly from the publisher. Send $12.95 plus $3.00 handling (check or money order) to: Mercurius Publishing, Box 156, Scottsdale, Arizona 85252 or call 602-949-6007, Fax 602-991-8387

TABLE OF CONTENTS

FOREWORD

Barry Cowger's new book, RECONSTRUCTING THE REAL YOU, APPLYING ASTROLOGY TO FAMILY PSYCHOLOGY, provides a long overdue and unique context for astrology that has not been met until now.

So much of current astrology, and so many astrologers today, have the need for an application of astrology to life events outside those immediately apparent in the horoscope itself.

For the most part the overall approach to astrology has been to interpret the individual's astrology through the horoscope alone without reference to life history. This type of interpretation seems to me to be simple-minded at best and dangerous at worst, as the would-be astrologer "learns" something from some random source and then applies this "learning" to a client whose actual reality and life story has never been considered or allowed for. As a practicing astrologer who has counseled thousands of clients, I know from experience the dangerous results of such an approach.

This is why Barry's book is so valuable. Beyond the fact that it is well written and comprehensive, it is also extremely well researched, incorporating the crucial subjects of birth order and family dynamics into an astrological framework. His practice as a professional astrologer has allowed him to observe, refine and augment his understanding of this vast and fascinating subject. This combination of psychology and astrology will lead to major contributions in the astrological field providing the astrologer with an indispensable tool through which to uncover and begin to comprehend the enormous impact of family life, birth order and astrology on the shaping and defining of individual adult identity. This topic of early childhood imprinting is especially important and timely in view of the current movement of major planets through Capricorn and Scorpio. Hidden family secrets kept for so long in the darkness of denial are being revealed. When the "manhole cover" of psychological repression is finally blown off, only knowledge and benefit will result, and the challenge then becomes the integration of our individual functioning and awareness. The astrologer can help to reveal the powerful, yet unacknowledged, elements that so forcefully shape our lives. In this spirit, Barry's book is to be highly commended and recommended.

Jeffrey Green
Vashon Island, Washington
Spring 1992

ACKNOWLEDGEMENTS

My deepest thanks and gratitude go to both Jeffrey Green and Jim Lewis who have been my two most influential teachers and guides. Without their help, encouragement, and insights in both my personal and professional development, this book would have never been possible. I also wish to thank Diana Stone, my friend, counselor, and colleague for her love and support over the years, and to Martha Christy, my brilliant editor who managed to craft the raw ideas and mass of research material of my original manuscript into what it has become today. And also for her technical guidance and emotional support throughout our association.

Others who have been very instrumental are, Margaret Nalbandian and Laura N. Gerking who gave me the forum (NORWAC) to first present and refine the ideas in this book. Also to Laurie Salmons, Pat Hesselmann and Terry Warneke of the Arizona Society of Astrologers; Dennis Flaherty, Bruce Hammerslough and Rick Levine of the Washington State Astrologers Association; Joyce Jensen of Astrological Insights; Jimm Erickson for his additional editing and insights; Jackie Hoag who gave me important and timely research material, and to Tom Bridges for his additional editing and input.

I also wish to thank those individuals who agreed to be case studies in this book and who have shared their life experiences toward the benefit and growth of astrology. And finally, a special thanks to Jan "Alexi" Lehn whose presence and support during the very first conceptual stages of this book was critical in both its initial unfoldment and subsequent development.

INTRODUCTION

"Wheels within wheels in a spiral array
  a pattern so grand and complex
  time after time we lose sight of the way
  our causes can't see their effects."
                                    Circa - Rush

Within the vast "stellar" pattern of our life experiences most of us, in a sense, have lost our way. Our own particular wheel of life spins through the great spiral of time within a solar system of experiences so complex and multi-dimensional, that to find a solid landmark from which to begin our journey of self-discovery is often our most difficult life task.

As in Dante's **Inferno**, we prepare for our long and arduous journey of self-exploration by searching for guides and tools to assist us towards the goal of discovering ourselves. These guides, traditionally, have taken the form of psychiatrists, psychologists, counselors and researchers who have devoted lifetimes to "mapping out" and comprehending the complexities and intricacies of the human psyche.

For many generations, we have relied on these establishment figures to delineate prescribed paths for us to follow as we pursue the development of our own individuality and social consciousness.

However, the decades of the 1980's and '90's have given rise to a plethora of new self-awareness and self-improvement techniques and therapies that add a new dimension to traditional "Freudian-type" psychology, and lend a broader, more spiritual aspect to humanity's search for individual identity and meaning.

The art of Astrology, in concert with many forgotten and esoteric self-help tools of the past, is currently experiencing a resurgence in our society, and has been repositioned as a valuable resource for increasing personal self-awareness. As an astrologer myself, I have witnessed the increased control that clients gain over their lives as a result of the added understanding and awareness that astrological insights provide them, and I am grateful that, in this turbulent era, we have been given access, once again, to ancient arts, such as astrology, that assist us in making our way through the maze of our own personal psychologies.

Unfortunately, just as any instrument of change is liable to abuse, so is astrology, when misapplied by well-meaning but short-sighted astrologers, who often randomly apply astrological truths out of the context of the client's entire life story. Our society is rapidly approaching the realization that no science, medicine or improvement technique can be truly effective unless it treats the **whole person**, which includes their past as well as present life events and circumstances.

For this reason, I focus on giving astrological readings which work in conjunction with the individual client's **total life experiences,** particularly those which occur during their formative years. The family experience and birth order positioning influence so much of a person's character formation, attitudes and behavior, that, in my opinion, no therapy or self-exploration technique can be used effectively without first considering the particulars of a person's family and birth order placement.

An in-depth look into a person's childhood experiences and family history gives innumerable clues as to how that person's astrological chart should be interpreted. This method makes it much more possible to avoid the "shot in the dark" effect of applying generalized or "cookbook" interpretations to individual horoscopes.

As an example, the fact that your sun sign is in Aries does not necessarily mean that you, as an adult, actually discover your individuality through forceful, extraverted pioneering and risk-taking. These natural tendencies may have been overshadowed, first, by the fact that your family's character was introverted, not outgoing, and secondly, by your birth order position as the second child in a family of three boys.

Within this type of family structure, your self-confident, outgoing, courageous Aries nature could have been repressed by fearful, introverted parents who decidedly favored your eldest Taurus brother (reflective, withdrawn) over you, because he was more "like them". Under these circumstances, you probably got bombarded with the verbal or unconscious parental message, "If only you were more like your oldest brother".

Needless to say, this would hardly have had the effect of making you feel good about your real, "the world is my oyster" Aries nature, so you may have compensated by repressing your natural instincts so as to become more like your shy, withdrawn, introverted older brother.

Now, as a result of your childhood repression, you have grown up to be a frustrated, subliminally angry and confused adult, secretly and passionately desiring to be a daring, innovative business entrepreneur, while in fact, you hold a supervisory position in a civil service job. Given this whole scenario, it would hardly be useful to you to be told that your natal chart indicates that you are a rugged, pioneering type, driven by raw instinctual energy. However, after examining the details of your family dynamics, it becomes clear that the expression of your natal Aries nature was denied as a child and young adult, ("Why can't you be like your older brother?"), and that you have made career and life choices based on your parents' and oldest brother's natal identities, rather than on your own identity needs.

Now that you are more aware of the particular dynamics of your situation, you may choose to develop a new career and life-style which is more expressive of your real Aries self.

Understanding family dynamics such as family character and structure, birth order, etc., is of utmost importance to both the astrologer and the client as background material for correctly interpreting the horoscope. **Reconstructing the Real You, Applying Astrology to Family Psychology**, was written to specifically address this issue. It provides an in-depth look at how family dynamics and birth order work in conjunction with astrology to form and fashion individual character and identity, and it explores the effects of family patterning on our natal or "real" identities.

In combining these two different, yet, I believe, highly compatible disciplines, (astrology and psychology), I have found that clients are able to integrate and utilize their astrology in a much more profound sense, because their astrological reading has been tailored to their **total** individual reality, rather than reflecting the bare "skeleton" of their basic horoscope or natal chart.

As a result, mothers seem to better understand their relationships with their husbands and children; unhappy business executives or office workers turn to artistic careers, realizing that they are playing out their family roles rather than pursuing their appropriate careers; men and women find constructive love relationships rather than the destructive ones they draw to themselves because of their negative self-images formed during childhood.

The benefits of applying astrology in a holistic sense have been so compelling and convincing for both my clients and myself that I felt the need to share these insights and knowledge with a broader world of professional astrologers and people in general who simply want to know more about themselves. Because the material in the book deals with often very intense or complex issues, I heartily recommend that you digest each chapter slowly and individually, in order to understand the full implications of the various subjects presented, which, in some cases, involve so many variables and so much explanation, that they are not readily absorbed by superficial skimming or browsing.

I am grateful for the opportunity to pass on the material presented here, and it is my hope that others will benefit, as I have, from this expanded view of the valuable art and language of astrology.

RECONSTRUCTING THE REAL YOU

APPLYING ASTROLOGY
TO
FAMILY PSYCHOLOGY

PART ONE

FAMILY DYNAMICS

CHAPTER ONE

"I DID IT YOUR WAY"
The Rules That Families Live By

The family—the most basic, fundamental unit of our society is described by Mr. Webster as "a group of usually related persons living under one head." At first glance, it seems like an easily defined concept. Yet do any of us really understand our unavoidably complex experience within this basic societal group?

However we define it or profess to understand it, I'm sure that most of us would agree that the impact of our individual family experience is utterly profound. Almost everything we are, we owe to our families—our personal identities, thoughts, beliefs, self-images and attitudes—all are the byproducts of our participation and experience within our own specific family group.

In 1953, Saturn and Neptune conjoined in the sign Libra. This important astrological conjunction reflected the dawning of a new era of increased awareness of the impact of the family on character and personality development. With this new perspective, we, as a society, began to question our assumptions that sick, troubled or socially maladjusted adults were somehow just born "bad" or "weak" or confused.

The introduction of the current concept that "we are what our families make us", has given rise to what many family psychologists refer to as "family systems therapy". This form of family psychology utilizes the belief that the behavior and attitudes of each individual member must be analyzed in the context of their whole family's beliefs, attitude and behavior. In other words, parents and family dynamics are primary factors in determining how children learn to behave and function in society.

Everything in the parents' psychology influences their children. Siblings, likewise, profoundly affect each other. Parents and society are now more fully realizing that, in order to have constructive and peaceful societies, we must have constructive and harmonious family environments.

Because our family experience is so integral a part of the fabric of our psyches, it is often a difficult task to separate ourselves enough from it to study it objectively, but doing so is a crucial step in defining who and what we. As we move beyond the ties of home and family, into our adult lives, we are confronted with our own individuality—we are not our mothers, nor our fathers, even though we are a product of them both.

Unfortunately, I believe that, traditionally, in most societies, who and what a child becomes is primarily determined by what the parents believe he or she should be—so, probably very few of us have ever truly individuated. This is lamentable in consideration of the fact that the more we define and mold ourselves as self-determined, clearly identified individuals, the greater becomes our personal ability to realize constructive growth, personal power and a sense of well-being and accomplishment within our own worlds. However, in my opinion it is never to late to start the journey towards self-realization.

One of the ways we can accelerate the process of defining our own "real" identity is by looking back and reviewing ways in which we may have been unconsciously, or consciously imprinted by our parents' attitudes, beliefs and values.

Today, more than ever before, we have access to methods of identifying and releasing damaging family facades, so that our real selves can show through and be redefined and openly expressed. Astrology, in combination with family psychology, can be effectively used as one such tool in this important process.

It is true that during the last century of intense analytical empiricism, astrology seemed to have devolved into something indistinguishable from gypsy fortune telling, however, this is no longer true. Astrology is now, once again, highly regarded by many as an ancient tool for self-exploration, and through it, we are able to observe the natural laws or energies that seem to govern and determine our personality, our preferences and the way that we individually function in our world.

The astrological horoscope shows how we view our own world apart from the circumstances into which we are born. The horoscope indicates the "filters" through which we perceive our world.

These days, we are all becoming more conscious of our dual natures. We have an instinctive nature, represented by our astrological natal chart, and an "environmental" identity, formed by our family and social interactions. Generally, the only way we truly become aware of these two identities is when they come into conflict—because our instinctive side is struggling for external expression against our repressive environmental patterning.

For example, you, as a person with a Sagittarius sun sign, and a Gemini Moon, have a natural inclination to be a teacher, or mentor; you are curious, playful, and intellectual and love travel, and philosophy. Why, then, are you feeling depressed and miserable and why have you chosen a career as a postal worker and a timid, conservative, stay-at-home, Cancer, Moon in Pisces girlfriend? Obviously, your current life choices have been made on the basis of someone else's desires or attitudes—but whose? A look back into the annals of your family history will probably solve the mystery.

Although a thorough study of the family phenomenon is a rather formidable task because of the nearly inexhaustible variety of family structures, there are dominant themes that appear to apply to family life in general. The first of these themes that we'll be examining is the system of rules and values that all parents use in governing the behavior of their family members. Simply stated, parents set up the "rules of the game" for themselves and their children and everyone is expected to play by them.

The "whys and wherefores" of every individual family's set of rules are probably infinitely complex, but for our purposes, we'll begin by stating that, for the most part, family rules are based on the parents' own beliefs and values, which they usually inherit from **their** parents' religious or ethnic rules, traditions and beliefs. On the other hand, some parents rebel against their family traditions, and so they define rules for their dependents based on their own personal sociological or philosophical attitudes and opinions.

Whatever the case, it is the application and consequences of these various beliefs or rule systems that ultimately determine how children develop and function in the family circle and in society. The importance of appropriate parenting has probably never been more stressed than it is today, but given the rampant social ills of this and previous eras, it is probably true that the majority of children grow up with moderately to severely inappropriate, and even destructive, family rule systems and belief structures.

Rule systems in some families can be so stringent, that it's a wonder anyone can survive them, much less successfully individuate within them. Parents who govern themselves by strict sets of religious, cultural or philosophic dictums can end up legislating every move their children make—bullishly directing them when to eat, what to eat, how to eat it; what to wear, how to sit, stand, speak; what to think, who to associate with, when and whom to marry and so on and so on. "Bullish" or deeply imprinted parental figures usually feel obliged to dictate their offsprings' every belief, attitude and behavioral function in order to insure that they will conform to the family's ethnic, religious, or cultural traditions and beliefs.

Unfortunately, in these situations, the children's developmental and sociological functions are dictated by the parent(s) without reference to the individual needs, choices or preferences of their offspring, who either helplessly embrace these parental patterns as their own, or find themselves embroiled in bitter family conflicts. If children rebel against their parent's beliefs and "upset the family apple-cart", they may find that they are hated and ostracized by other family members, while fighting their losing or "bloody" battle for self-determination and identity.

In that most children feel a need to be approved, loved and accepted by their parents and relatives, they go along with the family agenda. Eventually, however, rigid and relentless family patterning superimposed over individual identity needs may result in severe repression, self-doubt, resentment, depression, and confusion, during childhood and into adulthood.

It goes without saying that this type of atmosphere is hardly conducive to constructive individuation. The family grouping, a phenomenon seen throughout nature, is intended to provide a nurturing environment within which the infant and young of a species are cared for and instructed in the art of successful adult survival and adaptation, thus insuring the preservation of the species.

If the raising of young is somehow compromised and the correct and appropriate survival skills are not properly transmitted, human dependents, just as dependents of other species, may be unable to make the transition to successful, constructive functioning once they "leave the nest", and ultimately, they may not flourish or even survive.

In the human community, much as we would like to consider ourselves as having transcended the laws of nature, we are governed by natural reproductive and survival laws, although, of course, our options for adaptation and survival are almost endlessly diverse. Because of this, and the fact that we are guided by cognitive thought in addition to our instinct, the guidelines for raising human children are, naturally, more complex and variable, having to conform to innumerable geographical, cultural, philosophical and social influences and variables.

Human parental figures most certainly are faced with a monumental task in preparing their children for successful adaptation and survival in the ever-changing, highly mutable, complex world to which they are heir, but I believe strongly that there is one common denominator relative to the raising of young which all species share in common, viz., the **instinct** to adapt and survive.

Unfortunately, human parents all too often fail to listen to their instincts and those of their dependents in the process of parenting, and thereby impose rationally derived, but inappropriate external rules and demands on their children which interfere with their natural individuation process.

For example, a child with a sun sign in Pisces, Moon in Cancer may instinctively prefer playing quietly at home alone or with one other child. Her parents, however, are both doctors and enjoy an extremely active social life, receiving a gratifying abundance of attention because of their successful standing in the community.

To them, their child's predilection for a consistent, quiet life at home appears aberrational, while, in fact, the daughter is simply responding **instinctively** to her own individual character impulses, and emotional needs, rather than to her parents'. Her mother senses that her child simply needs to follow her own course, but rejects her "gut" feeling about what is right for her daughter because of her husband's and her own rationalizations that their social identity and skills "work for them" and will therefore "work" for their child.

The parents in this case refuse to allow the child to fulfill her own needs and desires by continually forcing her into highly charged and challenging social situations which **they** consider indispensable "lessons" in adult living, but which terrify and overwhelm their daughter. This parental "force-feeding" creates all kinds of emotional problems for the daughter in childhood, and later, in her adult life, as she wrestles with the conflict between her own individual instinctual needs and desires and those of her parents.

This scenario illustrates the problems in the process of individuation that can occur when external parental rules, attitudes and beliefs are allowed to override, or fail to support the natural survival and adaptive impulses of the child.

Astrology, which can provide a child's natal "picture", can be particularly useful in parenting because it promotes a better understanding of what each child instinctively needs and desires in their developmental environment. Once parents better understand these specific identity differences in their children, the rules and dictates of the household can be modified in order to appropriately channel, rather than repress or distort each child's natural inclinations.

It is a parental fallacy that children are just "blank pages" that must be inscribed with a panoply of socially "correct" character traits in order to manufacture a productive societal member. While it cannot be denied that children must have careful, guided instruction in the art of successful living, it is, nevertheless, counter-productive to refuse to acknowledge that each child is born with certain character or temperament traits already in place. Astrology has been used throughout the centuries as a means of identifying natal character elements and, is therefore, an important tool that I believe needs to be integrated into child and family psychology today.

Currently, the term "dysfunctional" refers to the family model which fails to successfully support the constructive individuation process of its' dependents. The dysfunctional family is generally characterized by extremes. Dysfunctional parents usually either establish overly rigid, uncompromising rules for their children which nearly strangle the individuality out of them, or, conversely, they fail to construct any clearly defined or enforced behavioral guidelines at all, leaving the children to more or less fend for themselves in the character formation and social adaptation process.

Naturally, there are as many gradations of these extremes as there are families, but in general, the lack of moderation, sensitivity to individual needs, and balance in the parental approach produces unbalanced children who, subsequently, become unbalanced "dysfunctional" adults, who cannot make the independent, informed decisions that are the foundation for a happy, productive, constructive and fulfilling life.

Family traditions, rule system and beliefs need to be directive, yet fluid and nurturing, providing guidelines for juvenile behavior without erasing or completely replacing the child's natal identity. A family grouping which provides this type of well-defined, yet modifiable approach to parental rules and beliefs, and that allows for the natural unfolding of individual character within secure, defined, yet alterable guidelines is today referred to as the "functional" family.

Perhaps one of the most obvious examples of the differences between functional and dysfunctional family rules is seen when a child within a family reaches puberty—the inevitable moment when even the most outwardly tranquil home can be ravaged by a "life and death struggle" between parent and teenager. At this juncture, the adolescent and the parents are literally forced into a confrontation with the child's impending separation from the family.

The teenager has to face the fact that he or she will soon be fending for themselves in the world at large and will need to draw on their character and identity strengths in order to attain fulfilling, successful careers, adult relationships and so on.

The adolescent has to decide, through a series of trial and error experiments, which of his or her identity and character traits will work best and most positively affect the outcome of their adult life.

Should the parents' own beliefs and value system be threatened by this pubescent drive towards individuality, one or possibly both of the parents may wage and perhaps win their own battles in this "war of independence", and force the adolescent into compliance with the family's uncompromising, and possibly dysfunctional behavioral edicts. These battles may interrupt or "dis-integrate" the child's natural adaptation and individuation process and result in adolescent confusion, resentment and repression that is carried over into adulthood, disrupting and distorting the person's relationships, career and life experiences and choices.

Many times, children who are torn by loyalty issues between their own character and their parentally manufactured identity, show a correlation to a Mars aspect in their chart during adolescence, (Mars represents warlike energy/power issues). If parents were to seek astrological counseling during this time, this Mars aspect would alert them to their teenager's intense need to define, and defend their own autonomy (Mars). Also, by reviewing their child's horoscope, the parents could better understand how their son or daughter is inclined to express their individuality and many family fights and misunderstandings could be eliminated.

At the other end of the "rules" spectrum, is the scenario of the dysfunctional parents who, for one reason or another, simply abandon their children to a lax, irresponsible lifestyle which incorporates little parental guidance and direction. Children from these home environments are forced to somehow piece together and define their own behavioral rules, beliefs and personal identities—most often by mimicking those of their peer group. The current, destructive inner-city juvenile gangs are reflective of the possible consequences of this type of family dynamic.

Adults who experienced this lack of parental guidance in childhood can benefit from an examination of their natal charts which reveal their birth nature and instinctual needs that were probably never previously recognized or expressed, but which could be used in formulating a more appropriate "game plan" for their adult life.

As we advance into adult living, we may often find ourselves held back or somehow hindered in our relationships or careers, by forces we cannot identify or pinpoint. We may attribute our difficulties to superficial or external causes: "I can't keep a job because my bosses are all unreasonable; my marriage broke up because my husband was immature; I'm always sick because I can't find the right doctor", etc.

In these situations, it can be of paramount importance to review and examine deeper reasons and causes behind the things that go wrong with our lives—in particular, the specific parental and family influences that shaped our identity, goals, attitudes and self-image. What were these factors and how was our personal development affected by them? Reviewing our family rules, parental beliefs and traditions can reveal many of the unseen, unrealized elements in our psychology which often govern our actions and life-events in frustratingly non-constructive and undesirable ways.

Unfortunately, it may sometimes be difficult for us to define exactly what our family "regulations" were and how they affected us, because not all rules are explicit. In other words, some family rules are verbally stated and defined for the children by their parents, and some are not. Many families, operate on the basis of implied rules which are never verbalized, but which each member recognizes and is expected to conform to, regardless of whether or not they understand the purpose and meaning of the unspoken rule.

For instance, an alcoholic father, when drunk, is routinely referred to as "tired" by his family. The mother and children implicitly abide by this unspoken "rule", even though it has never been verbally expressed, but rather, was solely conveyed by the mother's insistent use of the term, accompanied by her reinforcing facial expressions, etc. The mother has never actually said to her children: "Please refer to your father as "tired" when he's drunk, so that none of us will have to honestly deal with the fact that he's an alcoholic", so the origins and purpose of this family rule might never be consciously understood by the children who are expected to follow it.

Using the term "tired" as opposed to "drunk" may seem appropriate to the mother as a way of maintaining family harmony, but this unspoken rule imposes a completely false reality on family members. No one in the family is allowed to "name" or honestly react to this serious threat to their family's healthy functioning.

Obviously, this type of unspoken acceptance and unconscious obedience to a negative or unrealistic family dictum can have deleterious effects on the psychological health and successful development of the children involved. In adhering to such an obviously inappropriate rule, the children are prevented from seeking constructive ways of coping with their father's alcoholism.

The children's non-constructive coping in this situation might take the form of self-blame, self-hatred, depression, anxiety or an inflated sense of responsibility. These attitudes, carried over into adulthood, will most likely adversely affect their careers, relationships, etc. However, because of the covert nature of the family "lie" that originally created the problems, it is all the more difficult for anyone to pinpoint the cause of the person's depression, anxiety, self-hate and so on.

Astrological inquiry into one's past or present family dynamics or rule system should also include an examination of the position and aspects related to Saturn in the person's chart. For example, a child whose horoscope shows Saturn in Aquarius or in the Eleventh House, may have an intrinsically rebellious nature which is extremely sensitive to any and all forms of external guidelines, rules, or limits, whether they are functional or not.

This does not mean that the child will never get along with his or her parents or any other authority figures, but it does suggest that the child may instinctively need to reject certain family customs and rules very early in their life in order to begin to experiment with their own identity and authority.

If the parents have little or no clue about this child's independent natal character and attempt to override the youngster's natural instincts by insisting on obedience to the "way we do things", the child can become extremely rebellious and resentful and may never want to listen to any constructive parental or social guidance.

The child may grow up feeling very anti-social, (Aquarius/ Eleventh House), and may "throw out the parents (and society) with the bath water", because the family rules and guidelines were too oppressive or limiting and did not allow for individual expression. This child as an adult, may negatively express his or her "rebelliousness" by always finding fault and feeling out of place with society, and might become a social activist, revolutionary or radical.

This "revolutionary's" younger sister, on the other hand, has Saturn in Libra and the Seventh House and she feels "chosen" to bring her rebellious Saturn-in-Aquarius sibling back into the family "fold". Because she is extremely sensitive to any disruption of the family's peace and harmony, she joins forces with her parents in the battle against her non-conformist sister and fights valiantly to maintain the family's status quo at the expense of her sibling's intense need for individuality and autonomy.

This is a good example of how a little astrology could go a long way. This family, after astrological and professional family counseling, could avoid a great deal of "bloodshed" and pain, by simply giving their non-conformist family member the "space" that she instinctively needs to express her strong natal sense of independence.

An angular (or dominant) Saturn, or planets in the Tenth House or Capricorn may suggest that an individual feels a strong pull to **conform** to their family's moral, social or behavioral injunctions, and expectations.

John F. Kennedy, for instance, was born under a dominant Saturn aspect. His eldest brother, Joe, was killed during John's Saturn Return, (around age 27), which resulted in John's becoming his father's (Saturn) replacement "candidate" for a politically powerful future.

Even though John's chart indicates that he was not "constitutionally" suited to positions of intense social responsibility (his Neptune conjoined his midheaven), his strong Neptune influence, made him all too susceptible to the false responsibility of having to fulfill his father's (Saturn) dreams and expectations.

A Neptune influence also suggests that a person may be seen as a storybook idol, and John F. Kennedy was the epitome of the Neptune "hero"—young, handsome, charismatic, rich and powerful—the consummate "prince" of his paternal empire. However, John's **willingness** to assume heavy Saturn responsibilities did not necessarily guarantee that he was also able to fulfill them.

In fact, his untimely death, I conjecture, may have come about as a result of his unconscious reaction to, and compensation for, his internal Neptune/Saturn conflicts: "I've got to live up to my responsibilities and my father's (Saturn) expectations, but I'd desperately prefer to just hang out at the beach (Neptune) and enjoy life."

Unfortunately, John may well have embodied the ultimate modern "Siegfried" or hero-archetype, whose life vividly illustrates the dire consequences of trying to live out someone else's dreams and reality. John Kennedy also represents the tragic "Icarus", who dramatically "crashes to earth" after "flying too close to the sun" (his father's world). John undertakes these awesome Saturn responsibilities all in an effort to please his father and to attain **his** astronomical goals—which, unfortunately were completely incompatible with John's own natal needs and identity.

One of the most important planets to aspect (influence) Saturn is Jupiter. Jupiter's house position and phase relationship to Saturn shows the way in which a person expands (Jupiter), or uses their family past (Saturn) in creating new traditions or beliefs of their own. JFK had Jupiter and Saturn in a Last Quarter Square, suggesting that the values and beliefs of his father (Saturn) had become "stale" and meaningless to him as his life progressed. JFK may have experienced his extreme life crisis because he failed to express and defend his own identity needs.

It is also important to observe if Saturn is retrograde in a person's chart. Saturn (family rules/beliefs) retrograde creates a need for people to define, **for themselves**, their own inner and internal reality (retrograde) as opposed to their parents' or family's. During this cycle, individuals may feel an inner resistance to accepting any external authority, and may try to overtly reject what they perceive to be arbitrary or limiting rules that restrict their behavior and self-expression.

Ironically, this positive drive towards self-definition in a Saturn retrograde cycle is often compromised by the fact that Saturn retrograde people usually have a rather weakly defined sense of personal identity to begin with, and can therefore, be unwittingly steered by others into a career, relationships or lifestyles that ultimately do not express their own individuality.

Persons with Saturn retrograde many times try to compensate for their lack of internal definition by setting up strict external standards for themselves and others, e.g., they try to be very religious, or very conscientious, or more productive, etc., etc. However, this compensatory behavior is usually doomed to failure because their Saturn retrograde is simultaneously **forcing** them to redefine and reconstruct their inner authority and identity, sometimes through a process of **intense** withdrawal from family and friends.

Parents of Saturn retrograde children should understand that they are ultra-sensitive to social standards of behavior, dress, food, education, self-expression, etc. Identity issues are often dominant concerns for Saturn retrograde children at a much younger age than for Saturn direct children, so it is very important that parents encourage and support their "retrograde" children to **internally** define their own likes and dislikes, rather than mimicking other people's attitudes and behavior.

Family myths are another type of parental projection that can interfere with children's appropriate character and identity formation. Family myths are usually developed out of the parent or parents' need to live out their own mental fantasies or fears through one or more of their children.

As an example, a mother who has not successfully individuated or mentally separated from her own parents, begins to experience intense feelings of anxiety and fear when her adolescent daughter is preparing to leave home for a new apartment and job. In response to these subliminal emotions, the mother begins to develop "myths" about her daughter which she may never have expressed before, and which usually have absolutely no basis in fact.

The mother now begins to verbalize her anxieties by predicting the negative consequences of her daughter's move: "Now, Jean, you've always gotten in trouble when you stay out too late, so I'll call to make sure you get home early", or, "You know you've never been able to get up on time, so you'll probably always be late for work", or, "I know you're afraid of being alone, so Daddy and I will always be checking up on you."

The daughter may be absolutely mystified by these inexplicable statements that seem to spring from out of "nowhere", but because she and her mother have an otherwise amicable relationship, she accepts these myths on some level as true. Unfortunately, these myths, or maternal projections, undermine the girl's sense of herself as courageous and grown-up, and considerably diminish her self-confidence as she moves into her new apartment and her new life.

More pervasive family myths involving, for instance, the children's career choices, can also be difficult to overcome: "John will be the banker, and Jeff will be the artist of the family". These statements predict the childrens' career outcomes even before they have had any opportunity to assess their own personal preferences.

It is a difficult and often insurmountable task for adolescents or young adults to extricate themselves from their roles in ongoing family myths. However, at the time of the Saturn Return, which occurs between the ages of 28 and 29, we usually all experience an emphasized "pulling away" from our cultural and parents' identities. This is also a period of accelerated maturation in which our own internal authority, values and beliefs are tested, experimented with, synthesized and hopefully integrated.

This Saturn Return cycle represents an excellent opportunity for a person to consciously examine and overcome any deleterious parental myths or fantasies which may have been unconsciously assimilated and integrated during childhood and early adulthood.

The house position of the planet Neptune, or planets in Pisces or the Twelfth house, are also important when reviewing family history, as they indicate a susceptibility to accepting and maintaining a family myth about oneself.

Arnold Mindell, a former Jungian analyst and pioneer in what is called "process psychology", has done fascinating work with what he calls the "dreambody" or the mentally projected mythical image through which a person's unrealized, and repressed desires and fantasies are acted out through another individual.

As an example of this "dreambody" concept operating in a family environment, a Sixth House Neptune daughter becomes the target of her father's career disappointments: "I never got the chance to have my artistic career." The father projects his frustration onto his daughter by openly discouraging her artistic inclinations: "Forget art, dear—you have to do something 'real' with your life." The girl, of course, begins to take on her father's "frustrated artist" issue and feels that she, too, has no right to or opportunity for her artistic expression, even though her family, unlike her father's, could well afford to support her career in art.

She becomes increasingly depressed, frustrated and defeated, and feels that "I can't be who I really am". She integrates her father's myth about her artistic opportunities and continues to act out her father's disappointments even into her adulthood, suffering from ill health, and emotional instability as a result.

For most young adults, family myths, rules and traditions are generally key factors in determining which career to follow. Adolescents who are in the midst of, or who are just completing their high-school education, are often apprehensive about making these important life choices and commitments. And well they should be, given the fact that most original career choices are made without any real awareness and understanding of the family dynamics that influence these decisions.

Unconscious integration of inappropriate family programming often results in career and lifestyle confusion and dissatisfaction that most adolescents do not consciously anticipate. Fortunately, there is now increasing emphasis on creating new, more appropriate parenting techniques, which, hopefully, will help create a new generation of young people who are raised in environments that truly foster self-expression, self-knowledge and constructive individuation.

Beginning in 1988, we entered into a 35-year cycle of a Saturn/Neptune conjunction in the sign Capricorn. This configuration represents the possibility of critical events that may occur when the "old" refuses to give way to the "new", and it heralded the beginnings of a huge cultural crisis in the United States related to the quality of child-rearing and family life in this country.

Many of us now realize that in order to create a stable, constructive society and world in the future, we must address the problems in our families today. We need to collectively admit that there is a dangerous domino effect that is created, when the unresolved problems of individual families "roll" into the larger collective or social consciousness (Neptune) of current and succeeding generations (Saturn/Neptune).

This snowball effect of negative family patterning, generation after generation, has created more and more sociological upheaval as the children of dysfunctional families are "dumped", with all their psychological schisms, into an already confused and struggling society.

Interestingly, John Bradshaw's landmark book, **The Family**, was released in 1988, when this Saturn/Neptune conjunction commenced. His book inaugurated a new era of close examination and reworking of the entire concept of families and parenting that is still ongoing and intensely relevant today.

During the remaining years of this Saturn/Neptune conjunction, we have a tremendous opportunity to reverse and heal the effects of our collective mis-perceptions and misunderstandings, (Saturn/Neptune), regarding parenting and family life. Rather than allowing the mistakes of the past to dictate our future, we can choose, in the light of our recent awareness, to take advantage of this present planetary cycle to raise the collective consciousness of our world, by correcting our entire psychology of parenting.

Succeeding generations stand to benefit enormously from the intense scrutiny that child raising and education is receiving today, especially if we take responsibility for this crucial issue and enact the changes that will insure that more families produce psychologically and physiologically whole children and adults for the preservation of our species.

CHAPTER TWO

THE PARTS THAT PEOPLE PLAY
Acting Out Assigned Family Roles

Most of us are familiar with the concept of role assignment and role-playing within the family. In any type of group experience, each participating member assumes a unique character or role through which he or she relates and contributes to the overall group—as Shakespeare so aptly put it: "All the world's a stage". And in fact, parents and siblings are the actors in their family "theaters", expressing their individual characters or temperaments through the roles they assume or are assigned. Typical family roles can include the "academic", the "jock", the "scapegoat", the "clown", the "baby" and so on.

Within a functional family, role playing can be a psychologically healthy and constructive technique in character formation; each child gets to act out or "try on" one or even a variety of "identities" in order to find the role that "fits", or, in other words, is most in keeping with his or her internal natal identity. This type of experimentation works well within the family if the parents are not threatened in some way by the roles which their children experiment with, but many parents are, in fact, very threatened, especially if the role playing begins to incorporate behavior which is in conflict with their own belief system.

Parents who feel the need to control their children through a rigid system of family rules and regulations, will also tend to assign equally rigid roles to each child. These roles are often based upon the needs of the family as a whole, rather than upon the individual desires of the children. For example, the eldest child of a large family, could be assigned the role of surrogate mother by her parents, while her younger siblings might be expected to assume other roles of responsibility such as housecleaning, peace-keeping, rule enforcement, disciplining, etc.

Imposing "fabricated" roles on children can have the same effect of imposing rigid, generalized parental rules and beliefs—the successful development of the childrens' individuality is compromised and subverted. The adult identity roles and attitudes that the children assume later in life may well not express their natal characters, but rather, represent a complex web of adaptive behavior constructed in response to the parents' expectations, needs and desires.

As most of us know, keeping up these "false" identities and concepts of ourselves through our adult lives makes it almost impossible to find truly fulfilling and appropriate careers, lifestyles and relationships. The explosive, radical behavior of the 1960's reflected the immense internal frustration and loss of direction that can result from the suppression of individuality by uncompromising parental and societal patterning.

More than any other "planet" in astrology, the Moon is focal in terms of which roles people will assume or take-in, in response to their childhood environment. The Moon represents our need to be touched, and nurtured, to feel warmth and support and to experience the world as a safe, secure place to be. Our first "Moon" needs are met by our parents, and as a result we want to please and obey them so that we can continue to receive their love and nurturing. An unfulfilled "Moon connection" with our parents leaves us feeling vulnerable, lonely, abandoned and afraid.

Because we need and want our parents' approval, and because our infant and juvenile ego-boundaries (Moon) and identities are not yet crystallized and socially integrated, we generally do not resist any type of parental patterning; we simply accept the values and identity roles that our parents, for any number of reasons, assign to us.

The Moon's house and sign position in a person's chart, as well as aspects thrown by other planets, can indicate how and in what ways a person might be attached to, or limited by, his or her assigned family role. For example, a person with their **Moon in a Fire sign or house**, who has been forced to accept a rigid, inappropriate family role, such as surrogate father or mother, might express their suppressed "fiery" identity through varying degrees of anger and rage. In extreme cases, the person might become physically abusive or violent, or use sex as an act of violence, all in an attempt to bring attention to their intense inner frustration and pain that resulted from having been "saddled" with an unbearable family role. This type of person, as an adult, may also keep continually on the move, in order to run away or escape from their inner pain and conflict, or to keep from being trapped in confining circumstances that mirror their child-hood "imprisonment".

The **Moon in any Earth sign or house**, might influence a person who has been forced to play an inappropriate role to withdraw from people and society altogether or to become obses-sively involved with "toys" or things such as money and rela-tionships, or to compulsively busy themselves with work in an attempt to remain "stable" and create a sense of predictability in their lives: "No one will ever take control over me again."

Individuals with their **Moon in any Air sign or house**, who are unconsciously acting out a false role, may feel disassociated from their own feelings or the world in general. They may feel continually restless, nervous, indecisive or detached, or may live exclusively in an abstract world of ideas rather than participating in a full physical sense in their daily activities.

Those with their **Moon in any Water sign or house** may react to inappropriate role patterning by feeling that they cannot get in touch with their true emotions, and they may attempt to stimulate their feeling or sensations through extreme methods such as eating disorders (bulimia, anorexia) or the use of mood altering substances (drugs, alcohol, sexual addiction, etc). "Spacing out" may also be a escape or survival strategy for this type of person.

The Moon in relation to each of the twelve zodiacal signs and houses is also an important and revealing element that should be consulted when dealing with the issue of inappropriately assumed roles or identities:

Moon in Aries or First House: suggests that a person may have an emotionally or physically absent mother figure, who was extremely uncomfortable with her role as a woman, wife, etc., or who lacked stability or consistency in her relationship to her children. If the mother is somehow absent, her daughter may take on the role of "wife" and become the father's sexual and emotional surrogate. As adults, people whose mothers were absent in one way or another in their childhoods, are often attracted to partners or mates who are like their mothers—emotionally unavailable or physically distant.

Accepting such an extremely inappropriate role as surrogate wife could also result later in life in irrational impatience or anger towards others, or fear of getting too close in relationships. The role of family rebel or overachiever may also be likely.

Moon in Taurus or Second House: The child may become the "lost" or depressed and apathetic family member when forced into false role playing. He or she may exhibit a strong tendency to withdraw from the family, to become isolated and wish "not to be." If female, the child may take seek out the role as surrogate wife or her father's confidant and strive to win her father's affection and attention, possibly inciting her mother's jealousy and wrath. The male child under this astrological configuration, as an adult, may express his love and affection exclusively through sex rather than through true emotion.

Moon in Gemini or Third House: This child may take the role as family "pet" or "mascot", in an attempt to divert attention away from the family's problems—such as lack of communication, feeling and emotion among family members. The child may behave hyperactively or talk compulsively in hopes of avoiding their own or their family's emotional pain. The absence of clear communication in the family may also produce a continual stream of mixed signals which can deeply effect the Moon in Gemini child by making him or her feel "crazy" or compulsive. The family may regard this child as the "Identified Patient" or the psychologically "damaged" member of the family.

Moon in Cancer or Fourth House: This person may assume the role of family caretaker, and attempt to act as the sole emotional support of one or both of the parents in a dysfunctional family. The child can become Dad's "buddy" and "champion", if female, or Mom's confidant and protector, if male.

Acting out this role often results in children becoming hypervigilant and fearful of possible catastrophic future events, or they may feel perpetually fearful of losing their "security" in general. However, these children can actually prefer this state of perpetual fear to having to confront or destroy their idealized images of their parents as "OK". Children in this situation may end up feeling everything in their lives too intensely without knowing why, or may feel nothing at all as a defense mechanism to deal with their fear. Compulsive eating disorders may also develop.

Moon in Leo or Fifth House: May produce the role of the family hero or the "chosen" child. This child can "do no wrong" in the parent's eyes and may become an extension of the parent(s) unfulfilled creative aspirations or goals. On the other hand, the child with this configuration, may assume the role of family "screwball", "outlaw", or dramatizer, in order to get attention or to distract the parents and family from real family issues.

Moon in Virgo or the Sixth House: A common role under this sign may be the hypochondriac of the family—the child who is always sick or in a state of continual crisis. Such children can be extremely sensitive and nervous, or perpetually apprehensive, having possibly bonded to their mother's fears and anxieties.

These repetitive illnesses are often real, and act as a method of drawing the family's attention to the lack of feeling, spontaneity or lightheartedness in the household. A female child under this sign may take the role of Mom's "scapegoat" or surrogate and take on her illnesses. These children may also assume the role as the family's "perfect child", or may under or overachieve in order to distract the family from its addiction or co-dependency issues.

Moon in Libra or the Seventh House: Children with this Moon sign assume the role as the family referee or peace-maker; they may feel that it is their duty to uphold their families' public images by insisting to everyone, within and without the family, that everything is "just fine"—whether it is or not.

This Moon in Libra child may also become the "darling" of the family, always smiling, laughing and animatedly relating in an attempt to disguise their own and their family's grief, sadness, anger or loneliness. Academic and social success is often achieved throughout adolescence, as the child struggles to be the family's co-dependent protector or enabler.

Many times, these children as adults, have a difficult time separating themselves from others, or in ending negative relationships simply because they have been programmed to believe that other's needs and desires take priority over their own. Eating disorders arising from suppressed anger are also common in this situation.

Moon in Scorpio or Eighth House: Suggests the possibility that the emotions, vulnerabilities, and needs of simply "being a child" may have been grossly violated, either emotionally or physically. These types of children may become the silent or withdrawn members of their families. Self-mutilation, self-destructive behavior, or eating disorders may become methods by which these children act out the dysfunctional family's "secrets".

In adolescence, they may act out their repressed instinctive Scorpio nature through sexual promiscuity or addictions which may mask anger toward the parent(s). Conversely, they may rebel against their feeling that they are controlled by their sexual nature and may become sexually inactive because of their fear of being violated, manipulated or abused, as they were in their family life.

Moon in Sagittarius or the Ninth House: May produce the role of family favorite or "genius", "Dad's hero", or "champion athlete". Or, on the other hand, a dysfunctional child under this sign may adopt the role as the family "distractor"—running away, withdrawing from other family members, etc., in order to draw attention to themselves and away from possibly explosive, emotional family issues.

Behavioral exaggerations, idealizing, dramatizing or forced optimism may also play a role here. As an adult, this often philosophical or idealistic person may become extremely self-righteous or religiously addicted, setting up and attempting to live by unrealistically high standards of achievement and accomplishment, (the Icarus Syndrome).

Moon in Capricorn or the Tenth House: These children, in a dysfunctional environment, most often feel that they do not receive the parental affection, attention or emotional support they need, and, in response, may assume the role of the super-responsible "white knight" or rescuer of the family in order to prove to themselves and others, their individual self-worth and personal value.

Occasionally, in the case of a domineering or intolerant mother, the child may act as the father's "defender" and ally, fighting his or her father's battles against the mother. Conversely, should the father be the perceived negative parent, the child may reject him altogether, and do battle against him on behalf of the remaining family members, all the while maintaining the family's public image of perfection.

Moon in Aquarius or Eleventh House: Within an emotionally repressed family environment, persons under this aspect may react to the lack or absence of emotional expression by becoming the family rebel, maverick or outcast. They may often feel on the "edge of sanity" and dissociated from their feelings and their own body. In essence, they mirror the emotional split in the family. Sleeping disorders and hysteria may also result as the child (and later, the adult), acts out the often intense inner tension and anxiety which can accompany repressed feelings and emotions.

Moon in Pisces or Twelfth House: A person under these aspects can be prone to mirroring the stresses, dependency needs or the vulnerabilities of family members or the family unit. This child will most likely bond with the mother's compulsive worrying, and victim approach to life.

The role of family victim or scapegoat can also result in this case, as well as the role of the "invisible" family member, who asks for nothing and requires nothing—reflecting the entire family's "numbness", and sense of hopelessness.

The scenarios and profiles described above are, of course, never "cut and dried". I use these generalizations as initial guidelines for pointing out a possible false identity or role that a person may have internalized as a result of their family patterning.

All of us adopt roles as children, in our families, and in other relationships as well, in order to maintain stability, consistency, security and predictability (Moon) in our interactions. These roles, for the most part, are indispensable tools that we use to function and grow. Conflict around the issue of role playing only arises when we assume and act out roles that repress or distort our instinctive identity needs.

Inappropriate childhood roles can follow us far into adulthood, long after our parents are gone. Unfortunately the effects of these character roles seem to live on forever, or at least until we are awakened to their existence and influence through some form of self-analysis.

I find that astrological analysis does assist in revealing the "hows" and "whys" of roles that people play, and when applied within the context of family history, can yield tremendous benefits and insights.

For example, a woman with a Scorpio Moon begins a relationship with a man whose Moon is in Libra. The woman, having grown up in an emotionally abusive family environment, tends to be generally silent and withdrawn, and is now feeling extremely conflicted and unable to participate emotionally and sexually in her new relationship.

She wants to express her fears and anxieties to her partner, whom she actually loves and admires, but he has adopted his Libra Moon "face-saving" role early in life, meaning that he wants to deny the reality and importance of his girlfriend's feelings so as to maintain the facade of stability and harmony in the relationship.

As the protector, or enabler of the relationship (Libra Moon), he responds to his partner's tears and emotional disturbances with phrases like: "Everything's fine, honey, it's all OK. I'll take care of everything". Rather than allowing her deep-seated emotional conflicts to surface, be expressed and dealt with, he tries desperately to assuage and cover up her emotional "aberrations" by acting-out, just as he did for his family, his "white knight" protector role.

The implications for the future of such a relationship are obviously dire for both partners, neither of which is able to allow the eruption or release of their harmful, repressed psychological material within the relationship.

In order to avoid misunderstandings like the one above, a simple dialogue with an astrologer about your Moon position and the role or roles that you assumed early in childhood can help you get in touch with your deepest security (or Moon) issues and patterns so that you will be more aware of the subliminal forces at work in your relationships.

The Moon aspect in our consciousness is a primary imaging factor—that is, it deeply influences the development of our self-image and identity. A review of your Moon position as it relates to your present role playing and identity can help you develop a new, more appropriate self-image that reflects your positive natal identity rather than the distorted character traits that were developed because of negative family patterning and environment (Moon).

"Cancer Moons", for example, who are accustomed to dependency on outside factors and persons for physical and emotional support can come to realize that this negative dependency role can be exchanged for the positive natal trait of self-responsibility which, in this case, means allowing and encouraging themselves and others to be more independent by releasing their fears of the unknown.

A Libra Moon can exchange his or her protector role for the "good listener" role, realizing that it is possible to hear and cope with other people's emotional conflicts without feeling responsible for creating or solving them.

Moving beyond our earliest coping and survival mechanisms allows us to become more fulfilled, better functioning and happier adults. In the arena of role playing, looking to our Moon aspects can reveal the hidden dynamics that overshadow and obscure the more constructive roles that we are most suited to play in our inner and outer worlds.

Larry and Mindy Miller

Earth & Spirit Inc.

754 Ninth St. Durham, N.C. 27705

Wonders of our Earth and Spirit
For Awareness, Well-being and Delite

OPEN
Mon.-Sat.
10 a.m.-6 p.m.
Sun. 11-4

(919) 286-4250

CHAPTER THREE

THE CIRCLE GAME
Centrifugal and Centripetal Families

Carl Jung, the eminent Swiss psychologist coined the terms "introverted" and "extraverted" in order to classify or type different personality approaches. The introverted individual is characterized by a withdrawn attitude and derives value, pleasure and meaning primarily from relating to the world inside themselves. Extraverts, on the other hand, find their reality in and derive their value in life from the outer world—projecting themselves with "gusto" into the social milieu that surrounds them.

This character phenomenon also applies to social groupings, and has recently been applied specifically to the family group by an American family psychologist, M.S. Perlmutter. Perlmutter refers to introverted and extraverted families as "centripetal" (introverted) or "centrifugal" (extraverted). Perlmutter felt that typing individual family groups in this way reveals a number of important influences that operate upon and mold the children raised within these two distinct family types.

Perlmutter noted in his extensive studies on family psychology that the most common characteristics of the centripetal family appeared to be: 1) more female than male children; 2) generally larger with four or more children; 3) closely spaced siblings—usually less than three years apart; 4) a working-class or "low" economic status.

The dysfunctional centripetal family seems to more or less "collapse" in upon itself. In the worst case scenario, it can be likened to the galactic phenomenon of the "black hole". The vortex of the centripetal family's energy "sucks" the family members inward, pulling them away from the influences of outer reality; they subsequently become intertwined in a web of mutual dependency and fear.

These types of family members may often wish desperately to develop their own individual emotional and creative powers, but are, instead, enmeshed within the "seething" collective mass of interdependent family emotions and feelings, which sometimes makes it overwhelmingly difficult to break free of the centripetal family's "gravitational pull."

A dominant mother figure is another commonly shared element in centripetal families. The mother usually operates as the central authority figure and prime decision-maker with the family group, and is deferred to as the central authority figure by the children. In this scenario, the mother may attempt to maintain her control as the head of the family by undermining her husband covertly, or by acting out the role of underdog or victim through chronic, recurring illness. Or, she may openly defy her partner's attempts to assert any type of control over family matters.

Naturally, this ongoing parental battle can create emotional chaos for the children, as each child becomes polarized or loyal to one parent or the other.

The dominant implicit and often explicit message of the dysfunctional centripetal family is that the family unit itself contains all the elements needed for the fulfillment of the members' growth, and emotional needs. Outer social systems and organizations are viewed with suspicion or even fear, while any personal relationships external to the family are dimly perceived, also appearing frightening or even menacing to the centripetal family as a whole.

An extreme example of the centripetal psychology is the Appalachian mountain "hillbilly" family type which is almost completely severed from communication with outside sources and society. Individual separation, self-identity and autonomy are strictly discouraged within these families because individuality constitutes, for them, a threat to family unity and identity.

Needless to say, the possessive, introverted, centripetal family psychology, even in its more moderated forms, contributes to confusion and dysfunction as the children move towards adulthood and experience the inevitable urge to "leave the nest". The purpose of the family is to prepare children for survival, and then release them **into the outer world**. The dysfunctional centripetal family attitude may interfere with this natural integration process.

This centripetal psychology is also often characterized by feelings on the part of the children that, no matter how hard they struggle for independence from the family, their lives are never really their own, and that everything they do or accomplish is somehow only an extension of their parents', (particularly their mother's) identity needs, rather than their own.

At the opposite end of the spectrum, the centrifugal, or extraverted family is externally oriented. Sources of reward and pleasure are perceived as existing outside, not inside the family. Common characteristics shared by centrifugal families include: 1) more male than female offspring; 2) smaller family groups (3 or less children); 3) longer age-gaps between siblings.

Each of these variables contribute to the centrifugal family lifestyle, however, more than any of these, a dominant father figure will almost always turn the family in the direction of the "outside" world. In many centrifugal families, the father is characterized as "Saint Daddy", the authority figure who can do no wrong, who is "out there", making money, saving the world, and being comfortably intimate with hundreds of people and associates.

The family may not actually know who "Saint Daddy" is, and may feel emotionally starved for contact with him, but his position, image and lifestyle are upheld by the family unit as a whole, and usually supported by a plethora of defenses and rationalizations by the mother.

Within the centrifugal family, male children often feel strong inner and outer pressure to succeed and attain social recognition; they usually feel that the burden for carrying-on the family values, achievements and productivity is their primary responsibility. As adults, especially in the absence of the father, the centrifugal male will assume responsibility for the stability and even the very survival of family members and the group as a whole.

A centrifugal, as opposed to centripetal psychology appears to do more to foster and promote the individuality and independence of the offspring, but actually, in the dysfunctional home, this is usually only done as a means of securing the outside world's attention and admiration which is the primary goal of the centrifugal family. Financial success plays a big role in this psychology, and as you probably guessed, most wealthy families are centrifugal, and extremely image-oriented.

In examining these two family types, it is important to note that, when combined with a balanced approach, both centrifugal and centripetal attitudes and behavior can enrich and enhance, rather than distort, the lives and characters of individual family members.

By creating moderated, flexible family environments and boundaries for their children, parents can avoid the harmful behavioral and personality extremes that stunt individual growth, and offer the positive aspects and richness of their own introverted or extraverted natures.

From an astrological point of view, the planets Mars and Saturn play an integral role in determining how a child will react to their family's centripetal or centrifugal personality. Mars energy is involved in the process of autonomy, through which we achieve independence and self-assertion. Saturn, conversely, represents the status-quo, or in this case, the maintenance of family rules, traditions and boundaries. Mars and Saturn in aspect (or "talking") to each other in a person's chart can indicate difficulties that center around loyalty to one's self-identity (Mars), as opposed to the imprinted identity they have inherited from their family programming (Saturn).

People whose charts contain Mars and Saturn in aspects such as a conjunction, (0°), semi-sextile, (30°), semi-square, (45°), square (90°), sesqui-square, (135°), inconjunct (150°), or opposition, (180°), may find it particularly difficult to establish their own self-identity and goals without repetitively acting out their family's philosophy, character and identity.

Looking at the Mars/Saturn aspects of children from centripetal families, their Mars, which represents the energy of independence and autonomy, is repressed by the Saturn, or father/family dynamic.

The lack of parental encouragement of individual growth in the centripetal family often is manifested in the childrens' lack of serious commitment towards their schooling, relationships, marriage or other formal social structures outside the family.

This implicit, overpowering Saturn message translates as "Don't leave the family; you belong in **here**, not out **there**." This is often the centripetal mother's attitude because she fears that she might be abandoned by her children. Many times, the centripetal mother will create illness or crisis in her life as a means keeping her children close.

Projecting her own worst fears, worries and pessimism (negative Saturn energy) can be another method by which the introverted mother prevents her offspring from expressing their own positive Saturn/Mars energy which, if expressed, could act as a catalyst to encourage the children's independence (Mars) and desire to move out into the world establish their own families (Saturn).

In the dysfunctional centrifugal family, children frequently find themselves negatively expressing their repressed Mars energy (autonomy, independence) through extreme anger, aggression and rage. They may insensitively dominate or treat their friends, mates or people in general, as "pawns", or "things" to be manipulated and controlled. In extreme cases, this negative Mars energy, carried over into adulthood from the centrifugal home, can manifest as sociopathic behavior, and even destructive or violent crimes may result. In such cases, learning anger management skills and how to balance Mars (autonomy)/Saturn (father, family) energies is critical.

Another common characteristic of centrifugal children is what is known as the "Atlas syndrome", or in other words, they feel that they have to "carry the world on their shoulders". However, if their Saturn energy, (meaning pressure or gravity in this case), becomes too great at some point, the centrifugal adult may "drop the ball" or fail in some overly dramatic way.

Public humiliation as a result of scandal, theft, etc., may be the way that these personality types act out their own extreme and unbalanced extraverted psychology or Mars/Saturn conflict later in life, or they may develop a "workaholic" lifestyle in order to avoid having to confront any part of their inner or spiritual reality.

Viewing the birth chart from the centripetal/centrifugal perspective can provide many crucial insights into the ways in which people can modify or change their behavior in order to more appropriately reflect and integrate their own natal personality.

As important as it is to analyze the family's mode of relating to the outer world, it is also important to look at the way in which the family group relates to its own inner world. This brings up the issue of internal family boundaries. Is each family member seen by the others as autonomous, independent and deserving of individual "space", respect and esteem? Or, does the family see itself as an homogenous whole, with nothing belonging or pertaining to any one individual member in particular?

From an astrological viewpoint, the Second and Eighth Houses (and any planets within these houses), often symbolize how family members interact with each other.

For example, persons with planets in their Eighth House tend to be much more sensitive and vulnerable to the attitudes and emotional atmosphere within the family. An Eighth House Mars, may suggest deep fears based on issues of loss, betrayal or abandonment. A child whose chart contains this astrological configuration may be very much in need of special attention and encouragement, love and nurturing from parents and siblings.

However, if the family's internal structure is such that the needs of all its members are lumped into one "collective" need for food, shelter, etc., with minimal emotional support, an Eighth House Mars child could experience heightened and even extreme emotions of betrayal and abandonment: "I'm not special to anyone", or, "I always feel like everyone is using me."

Realizing and respecting the boundaries of each individual family member is an important part of parenting. These psychological spaces between family members help promote the children's separate identities so that they do not become enmeshed. Lack of family "spacing" may result in the children developing "yes-man" or submissive attitudes. They may also tend to over-identify with other people's feelings or have an over-exaggerated sense of responsibility for other people's problems.

The Second House is also involved in this issue. However, contrary to the Eighth-House influence which is more concerned with how people relate to others, the Second House represents a person's self-relation, or the tendency to withdraw from outside influences, into an inner, personal reality. Second House types often form strong, safe relationships to their inner selves, which compensates them for the loss of personal identity within the family.

I have noticed in my own work that many Second House adult children of dysfunctional families have remained "intact" in the face of intense childhood traumas, in contrast to Eighth House types, with a similar family past, who suffer obvious emotional, psychological or physical damage.

In doing reconstruction work for those from dysfunctional centripetal and centrifugal families, it is important to focus attention on the Second and Eighth Houses, noting what each indicates about the way in which a person has responded to his or her family interactions and lack of personal space. Promoting and emphasizing positive Second House energies of self-reliance and self-respect can be extremely helpful to traumatized Eighth House persons, and conversely, Second House "tough-it-through" types can benefit from fostering the sensitive, positive, vulnerable aspect of the Eighth House: "It's OK to trust people".

Investigation into our Mars/Saturn family dynamic as well as Eighth and Second Houses influences, can reveal a wealth of insights into our own individual personalities. Many of us have not clearly defined whether we ourselves are introverts or extraverts, because we are so busy acting out our parents' or family's personality.

In conjunction with the many forms of psychotherapy and self-awareness techniques, "horoscopic exams" can also offer very specific and useful information about how and why we developed the personality we manifest today.

PART TWO

THE BIRTH ORDER PHENOMENON

CHAPTER FOUR

BIRTH ORDER RULES ALL

In a 1970, **"Psychology Today"**, article entitled, "Birth Order Rules All", Walter Toman, an eminent Austrian psychologist and family counselor, described the results of his 10 year research project on birth order which involved 2000 German and Swiss families, 32 well-adjusted and divorced couples and about 700 other single individuals.

Toman concluded from his study that gender and birth order, (or rank) within the family of origin, are crucial determinants of personality and perception. Additionally, Toman noted that marriages or adult romantic relationships succeed most often when they duplicate the same birth order positions that each person in the couple experienced in childhood.

While I do not agree with Dr. Toman that birth order and gender determine everything we are as adults, I have seen for myself in working with people on their astrology and family history, that these variables do appear to play an extremely active, significant role in personality, identity and character formation.

The horoscope is a symbolic representation or picture of our natal identity, character elements, preferences and inclinations. However, all of these birth characteristics evolve and change as we move through our lives within a vast, complex network of family and social conditioning. More often than not, our "real" or natal, instinctive identity, as indicated in our horoscope, is obscured or is repressed by external imprints which reflect the psychology and influence of our parents, teachers, peers, and our birth influences.

By reviewing a variety of developmental factors that impact our lives, I hope to better enable astrologers and their clients to view the horoscope spherically, so that their astrological readings will add a deeper meaning and relevance to their lives as a whole.

Approaching astrology from this spherical perspective brings hidden meaning and facts about a person's psychological and emotional needs to the surface of conscious awareness. This broader contextual interpretation of the horoscope can help the astrologer to avoid the sometimes superficial readings that give people an oversimplified picture of their astrology's relationship to the other events that were or are occurring in their lives. Interpreting the natal chart within the overall perspective of the person's family past and environmental influences lends a more comprehensive, and I believe, more beneficial aspect to horoscopic interpretation.

In keeping with the spherical approach, we're going to add birth order to our already burgeoning list of environmental influences. Given that it is an extremely complex environmental and behavioral study, even before blending it with astrology, I've divided specific birth order scenarios into separate chapters so that they will be easier to work with.

In an attempt to simplify this formidable subject that defies simplicity, we'll begin with a few generalized examples of how the birth order theory works, utilizing information from the studies of Walter Toman, Freud, Adler and other birth order authorities.

And to make it even "simpler", we'll be using Toman's abbreviated coding system, or what I call the "familygram" which provides a somewhat more manageable method for discussing birth order relationships.

The familygram is simply an abbreviated sentence that works in this way: "B" and "S" represent brother and sister, respectively. The elder brother or sister precedes the younger sibling(s) in the equation; marriages are indicated by a slash (/). The brother's family and sibling constellation is on the left in the sentence, the sister's is on the right. If the couple has children, they will be indicated by a corresponding "B" or "S" in the middle of the diagram, between two slashes. The person(s) whose birth order is being examined is **not** enclosed in parentheses.

Let's begin with the example of a family that is composed of an older brother of a younger sister. The older brother's birth order position is abbreviated as **B(S)**. This older brother— B(S)—marries the younger sister of an older brother **(B)S**. This would actually be considered an "ideal" marriage by birth order experts, because the partners are getting the same peer relationship that they experienced in childhood in their respective families.

The older brother, in this example, is accustomed to living with a female who is his junior. His wife, (the younger sister of an older brother), is used to living with an authoritative older male sibling. In this case, there would likely be no conflicts over the husband's traditional "seniority" position. Additionally, since both of them are accustomed to living with a person of the opposite sex, there will be little or none of the "culture shock" that can occur when one or both marriage partners have not previously experienced living with members of the opposite sex in their childhood and family life.

In continuing with this couple's familygram, let's assume that they later have two children, first a boy, then a girl. Their familygram now looks like this: **B(S)/BS/(B)S**. This again, is an "ideal" family structure, because the children's birth order positions exactly mirror their parents' own sibling backgrounds, (older brother, younger sister), which makes it easier for the parents to anticipate and understand their children's sibling relationship.

A less ideal family structure would be an older brother of a sister, B(S), married to an older sister of a brother—**B(S)/S(B)**.

Here, the marriage partners are confronted with a living situation which is the direct opposite of what they experienced throughout their youth.

This relationship might well develop into ongoing fight for authority and dominance, as the wife attempts to control her husband in the same way she "bossed" and cared for her younger brother. The same is true for the husband in this relationship who expects his wife to conform to the more submissive attitude and behavior of his younger sister. Fortunately, this couple does have the advantage of having been exposed to cross-sex sibling relationships as children, which makes it easier for each of them to accept each other's gender differences, however, their opposite birth order positions can certainly create difficulties in their marriage.

Astrologically speaking, this couple's authority or power issues might be overshadowed by the planet Saturn. In this situation, Saturn is likely to indicate that both the husband and wife will have a deep fear (Saturn) of being unjustly judged or wronged (Saturn) by the other. Consciously or unconsciously, each may attempt to put the other in a subservient emotional or psychological position, because both are accustomed to being the authority figure who needs to be "right" and they are threatened by each other's drive for dominance in the relationship.

An interesting twist in this scenario might be a situation in which both of these elder children are "fed up" with the responsibility of being authority figures in their families, and, after marriage, they battle each for the subservient, submissive role in the relationship, each desiring to be taken care of by the other.

Firstborn siblings do need to be aware of their tendency to feel overly responsible for others; the firstborn or oldest child's drive to take charge and get the job done can be extremely productive within a relationship, but only if it is balanced with an acute conscious acceptance of their own emotional and psychological needs.

In another birth order example, a younger brother of an older sister marries an older sister of a younger brother—(S)B/S(B). They eventually have a son and a daughter—(S)B/BS/S(B). In this case, the parents may find it difficult to relate to their children on a number of different levels.

For instance, the father, as a younger brother, has been taken care of and possibly dominated by his older sister, and as a result may not be as strong enough role model for his son, who is an eldest brother. The son may see his father as weak, indecisive and dominated by his mother, who was herself the elder sister to a younger brother, and therefore probably the dominant authority figure in the marriage.

The son, in this situation, may experience feelings of disappointment and anger towards his mother, resenting her control over his father, meanwhile, experiencing frustration and shame because of his father's perceived "weakness".

On the other hand, the daughter in this family may well be pressured by her parents to take leadership and authority positions within the family, at school, and in her career. While little is expected by either parent of their son, (both parents being accustomed to the sub-dominant younger brother role), the daughter is heir to many parental achievement and leadership expectations.

The daughter in this family structure will most likely experience a loss of respect and esteem for her submissive father. Should she have an astrological configuration in her natal chart such as Saturn in the Twelfth House, (invisible father), for instance, her critical attitude towards her father would be accentuated.

In another hypothetical family, parents with the same sibling order—B(S)/(B)S —(older brother of a sister marries younger sister of a brother), have three children: a girl, then a boy, followed much later by another girl—B(S)/SBS/(B)S.

Again, the father and son may experience tension in their relationship because the father, as an older brother, is unable to comprehend the more submissive attitude of his son who is a younger brother. On the other hand, the eldest daughter, who feels a strong firstborn need for responsibility and leadership roles, gets no under-standing or sympathy from her mother, who is a younger sister of a brother and welcomes, expects and appreciates care and guidance from a dominant man.

With the birth of the third child, (the second daughter),the family dynamics change. At this point, the parents experience an unconscious, but definite feeling of favoritism towards the two youngest children, who now mirror their own sibling experience. Their son, like his father, is now the elder brother of a younger sister, and their youngest daughter is, of course, like the mother, the younger sister of an elder brother.

The eldest male child in this situation, (who was the youngest child before his sister's birth), suddenly "gets his act together", delighting in his new authoritative position in relation to his baby sister. However, the eldest sister in this situation gets "left in the dust" as it were, unable to fulfill or express her firstborn responsibility and power role in the family.

Unappreciated and ostracized by her parents, and possibly now defied and resented by her younger brother because of his new-found older brother authority, this eldest firstborn daughter could certainly experience a great deal of pain, rage and birth role frustration— overall, a confusing and disturbing childhood, which later undermines her self-image, self-esteem, career, relationships, etc. Mars (autonomy) and Saturn (family) are often found in dynamic aspect in such a case, indicating the need for claiming and defining one's own autonomy and identity in relationships, without anger or aggression.

This example underscores the crucial effect that the addition of new family members can have on the whole family environment. In reviewing a person's birth order information, it is particularly important to note births, deaths or departures of family members, because the entire family dynamic and interrelationship can be radically changed by such events. Family members can experience extreme stress or emotional disturbance if the situation is not properly integrated into the family psychology.

One of the "worst case" birth order scenarios in a relationship or marriage arises when both the partners are the same birth order and come from an identical monosexual sibling configuration. In other words, an eldest brother of a family of all male children marries an eldest sister of an all female family. Now the fireworks begin. Both partners, as eldest children, are struggling for dominance in the relationship, while neither of them can "bear" the gender differences of the other. And added to all this, most firstborns have a tendency to stereotype (Saturn) or idealize their partners. The husband and wife, in this case, will be committed to changing each other and may try to force their mate to conform to the imaginary, or idealized image which each holds for the other.

If this unfortunate, (only kidding), couple were to have children, they might both feel that they have at last gotten their longed for "juniors" to dominate. However, again, there might be an ongoing struggle for dominance between the parents, which would confuse their children by forcing them to take sides with one warring parent against the other, none of which would foster or promote family harmony.

This is not to say that a family such as the one I've just described is doomed to failure, however, family counseling that deals with birth order issues would certainly be invaluable here.

Children from a background like this one may tend to become "parentified". This means that the children feel more emotionally mature and responsible than the parents.

In one case that I dealt with, a child of about 10, I noticed that his chart showed a Capricorn rising, Moon in the First House, opposite Saturn in the Seventh House. This configuration is a classic indication of the "parent-identified" child. In this case, the child was the offspring of parents whose familygram looked like this: (BB)/B/(SS)S. In other words, the father was the younger brother in a family of all male children. The wife was the younger sister in a family of all female children. In this example, both parents are struggling, not for power or dominance, but rather, for "juniority" rights. Neither of them is willing to take the authority role in the family. Gender differences are also a potential problem here, because both parents grew up without exposure to opposite-sex siblings.

The child born into this type of parental relationship can be at great emotional risk because neither parent really desires or is accustomed to assuming the responsibility and authority of the parental role. In our example, neither parent wanted parental responsibility. Their ten-year-old son assumed the role of parenting himself, and a good translation of his attitude towards his parent would be his statement, "Mommy and Daddy, when are you going to grow up?"

The boy's Capricorn rising probably increased his critical attitude towards his immature parents, and his Saturn in the Seventh House appeared to encourage his inclination to assume the responsible (Seventh House), fathering (Saturn) role in the family. His First House Moon opposite his Saturn suggests the "war" or opposition between the mother (Moon) and father (Saturn), which the boy tried to reconcile by "taking over" (Capricorn) the parental role for them.

This case also brings up the issue of "only" children of dysfunctional parents. The only child will often be the target of the parents' projected insecurities and problems, or they may become "triangulated" in the parent's relationship and take on a surrogate husband or wife role, which exposes them to inappropriate sexual intimacy with the parent of the opposite gender—a potentially damaging psychological complex commonly known as the "Oedipal complex".

It's interesting to note that Freud, the oldest and for some time only child to his mother, was very much concerned with the relationship between parent and child, and the dynamics of the Oedipal complex, whereas, Adler, a fourth-born child, developed his psychology around sibling and social relationships, and related status and power issues.

Now let's gather together a few of the innumerable family history and birth order variables that we've already reviewed, blend them with a few astrological insights and see what we come up with.

We'll first review the hypothetical scenario of a troubled married couple who come for astrological counseling. Both partners agree that their relationship has been extremely strained because of their many inexplicably fierce, explosive arguments and fights. However, they really love each other, and are both committed to discovering the real source of their disagreements so that they can save their marriage.

The astrologer asks about their birth order positions: the husband is a younger brother of an older sister - (S)B, the wife, a younger sister of two older brothers - (BB)S.

On examining their respective natal charts, it appears that the husband has an Aries Sun and a Pisces Moon. The wife has a Taurus Sun and a Sagittarius Moon. The astrologer's initial look at the couple's charts produces an image, in his mind, of the Aries ram and the Taurus bull butting heads 'till the cows come home.

However, after taking each partner's family history and birth order information, the astrologer uncovers a whole new, and much broader dimension to the dynamics of this relationship.

The husband, as a Pisces Moon, and as the younger brother of a caring, nurturing older sister, has a sensitive emotional nature,

(Pisces). He enjoys his more passive younger-brother relationship with his wife in their intimate and personal life, however, his strong Aries Sun encourages him to assume the role as the dominant, decision-making head of his family.

Also, his father was an eldest child, and was critical of his loving, passive, younger-brother attitude towards his older sister. As a Pisces Moon, he was extremely sensitive to his father's criticism and he compensated for his father's disapproval by emphasizing his aggressive (Mars) nature, and hiding his affectionate, receptive Pisces nature. As an adult, he often bullishly "grabs" positions of power and authority in his career and relationships.

His wife, as the younger sister of two older brothers, should at first glance, feel comfortable with her husband's drive for dominance and authority. However, a recital of her family history reveals that her two older brothers were both sent away from home to attend boarding school when she was 11 years old, leaving her to take the family role as the eldest sibling to her two younger sisters.

Additionally, her father was an alcoholic, and her mother was an extremely domineering eldest sister of a younger brother. As a result, she had been forced to take on a tremendously over-exaggerated burden of responsibility, acting out the role as the surrogate mother for her birth family in response to her domineering, but emotionally disturbed mother's demands and her alcoholic father's absence.

In taking all of these family history and birth order factors into account, the astrologer and the couple receive a tremendously expanded view of the elements that are contributing to the authority issues in the marriage.

On the one hand, the wife is receiving conscious and unconscious messages from the husband that he welcomes being taken care of and nurtured by her, and, because of her childhood role as a surrogate mother, she is accustomed to doing this. Also, as a Taurus, she has the determination, "groundedness" and emotional strength necessary to assume the dominant authority role in her marriage, just as she did in her family of origin.

Because the husband's Pisces vulnerability appears to be an open invitation to the wife's dominant mothering behavior, she is surprised and offended when her take-charge attitude meets with her husband's Aries aggression and need for autonomy, at which point, they both explode with rage, anger and frustration.

In fact, the accustomed-to-controlling Aries husband, assuming that his wife understands that he's the "boss" and that his submissive attitude applies only to specific domestic decisions (like deciding on what to have for dinner), and moments of intimacy, is horrified and affronted when she asserts her authoritative, dominant mother role.

The resulting clash of wills, misunderstanding and strangled communication does indeed make for an eruptive home life for this pair. However, with counseling and communication, it can be dealt with, once the partners become aware of the underlying astrological, family and birth order issues that are affecting their marriage.

The Aries/Pisces younger-brother husband can now communicate with wife about his need for more clearly defined boundaries between their warm, caring, intimate life and his more aggressive role as the head of the family and his business. Likewise, the Taurus wife can verbalize and claim her need for a well-defined area in the marriage which allows for expression of her decision-making abilities and authority.

Each of the partners can become more sensitive to the other's vulnerabilities. The husband can offer additional emotional support to his wife in order to relieve her of her firstborn "I'm responsible for everything" feelings, and he can moderate his overly aggressive Aries/Mars energy with a softer Pisces approach. His wife can offer encouragement and support to offset her husband's fears of being seen as weak or vulnerable when expressing his caring, receptive side.

Another important aspect of the birth order phenomenon that I'd like to cover in this chapter is the issue of age spacing among siblings. Alfred Adler, one of the most quoted authorities on the psychology of birth order, noted that psychological effects of birth order are radically different depending on the number of years between siblings in a family.

When siblings are close in age, the characteristics of their respective birth order positions are dramatically emphasized. This is because the siblings interact more often and more intensely than they would if they were separated by a large age difference. The "pecking order" phenomenon is extremely important in closely age-spaced families, and well-defined birth order roles give each child a sense of "knowing their place" as they interact with their ever-present siblings.

As an example of how age-spacing can change birth order roles, a youngest girl in a family of three is eight years younger than her next oldest sister, and the eldest child in her family has left home before she was born. This child may be cast in her natural birth order role as the baby of the family, but she will also tend to be treated as an only child by her parents, rather than as the secondborn of three children, because of the significant age difference between her and her two older siblings.

When reviewing someone's birth order role, take the age-gap element into account before making conclusions about someone's birth order psychology.

The 1982 issue of **Journal of Marriage and the Family** cited a study of the effects of age-spacing on the development of self-esteem in children. The test subjects were 2,200 middle-born adolescent males. The results of the study suggested that middleborns have a significantly lower self-esteem than firstborns and lastborns within the same families.

The study also indicated that the self-esteem of these middleborn males was considerably lower when they were separated by only two years from their other siblings; those with sibling spacing of three to four years had significantly higher levels of self-esteem. I found this study to be interesting from an astrological point of view, because it takes approximately two years for Mars (which reflects the experience of and need for independent identity formation), to transit through one astrological cycle and return to its original position in the natal chart. Siblings born approximately two years apart often have their Mars conjoined (in synastry analysis), which can emphasize their individual (Mars) identity differences, and create an exaggerated sense of competition and identity confusion between them, which, if unchecked, may damage their sibling relationship.

In general, birth order research suggests that age-spacing of three years or more between siblings is most advantageous, as the characteristics of the corresponding birth order positions are less emphasized and less likely to interfere with individual self-expression than they are when there are only one or two years between siblings.

Other studies have suggested that close age-spacing is detrimental for males, while larger age-gaps are "bad" for female children, so this can be another factor to look at when considering how a person may have been affected by the age-spacing in their family of origin.

I have devoted a large portion of this book to the birth order phenomenon because I have discovered for myself that the more we understand about birth order, the better able we are to analyze and comprehend our family psychology and to apply our astrological knowledge to improving our everyday lives.

Having reviewed a considerable amount of generalized information on birth order and its role in astrological counseling in this chapter, we'll move on in the succeeding chapters to a closer examination of the dynamics of the birth order positions and how they work within different family environments.

CHAPTER FIVE

TWO-CHILD AND "TILTED" FAMILIES

The two-child family is a fairly easy unit to analyze in terms of each child's birth order positions, (a firstborn and a lastborn), provided that the children are age-spaced within two to four years of each other.

If the two siblings are spaced by more than five or six years, each child would tend to assume an only-child role, in addition to their first or lastborn role.

In a two-child family, the children, especially if they are the same sex and closely spaced, may try to separate themselves from each other by becoming complete opposites. In this situation, individuality can become an even bigger issue than it is ordinarily, because each of the siblings are vying with each other for separate self-identity.

Because they are so often "lumped" together by their parents, "You two are so much alike", two-child family siblings may deeply resent each other and they may make their individual identity choices based on nothing more than their perception of what their sibling would **not** choose. They are also likely to be constantly competing in an effort to outdo each other in school, social activities, career, marriage, etc.

Richard Galbraith, another authority on birth order, describes this two-child family dynamic as "sibling de-identification". This is the method by which two same-sex, closely-spaced siblings attempt to define their separate self-identities by adopting character traits or opinions that are distinctly different or opposed to their sibling's.

The problem with this process is that each child may develop their identity by default. In other words, identity and personality choices should be made on the basis of what works best or is most appropriate to the individual, whether or not those choices happen to coincide with a sibling's preferences.

This process of de-identification, if left uncorrected, can result in serious identity and role confusion later in life, because the children have selected character traits, values and beliefs at random, driven by their resentment of their sibling, rather than by their own natural inclinations, emotional make-up and identity needs.

Sibling rivalry, even though it may operate unconsciously, can become an insidious and destructive force in this two-child relationship, as the siblings each "scramble" to assert some form of self-identity, rather than discovering for themselves who they are in their own right.

The individuation process, even under the best possible circumstances, is always a delicate and endlessly intricate procedure. Under these adverse circumstances, the process can be seriously jeopardized or damaged. Naturally, these types of problems can occur in any family, but the tendency for it to occur is increased in the two-child family because of the close, one-on-one proximity of the siblings, and the polarization (or opposition) to which the pair is prone.

As an added note, the second child of a two-child family often has a particular advantage over the first in that he or she has more role models to choose from (mother, father and sibling); also, second children may be better able to express themselves because they feel less parental pressure to conform to societal opinions than their older sibling, who as the eldest child, may be more vulnerable to parental and social expectations.

Speaking astrologically, people who are more likely to be involved in this type of two-child dialectic are those who have planets in Libra or the Seventh House, or planets in Pisces or the Twelfth House. The Seventh House and the sign Libra correspond to how people evaluate and compare themselves to others: "Am I prettier, smarter, thinner, fitter, and more interesting than she is?" "Do I have a better job than he does? Should I go back to school so that I can get more respect on the job?"

For example, a man from a two-child family with a same-sex closely-spaced sibling has a Seventh House Pluto, and three planets in Aries in his Third House. This man would almost certainly qualify as someone who has felt the need to differentiate from his sibling. The

Seventh House Pluto suggests a possible present and past karmic pattern of developing self-identity through relationship issues (Seventh House), rather than through independent self-exploration.

People, and in particular, two-child siblings, who have the astrological configurations mentioned above, need to be encouraged and empowered to find their own life-course, identity and destiny (First House) which are not dependent on other people's judgments or values (Seventh House). Transits and progressions to the First House and by First House planets should also be looked at when dealing with issues of self-discovery and individual identity, particularly for persons from two-child families.

In our previous example, the man's Aries planets suggest that he may be driven, in his present life, to try and break free from his tendency to compare himself to others and to evaluate his life and achievements based on those comparisons. His two-child sibling relationship mirrored this dynamic.

On the other side of the issue, planets in Pisces or the Twelfth House may suggest that a person is unconsciously mirroring or reflecting a sibling's lifestyle and values—over-identifying, as opposed to de-identifying with their brother or sister in a two-child family environment. This type of a person may feel that they have no life or direction of their own. People with planets in Pisces may often experience serious life crises as a result of this internal identity confusion.

However, as in all cases, no one should make assumptions about a person's life or psychology solely on the basis of their astrological configurations. Try to consider the horoscope in the light of the many other factors in the person's life and history in order to avoid sometimes dangerous over-simplifications of complex emotional or psychological issues.

Another important family type is the "tilted" family. A family is considered to be tilted if all the children are the same gender. Technically, an only-child family is also considered tilted. Because there has been an increasing trend towards smaller families in recent decades, the chances of having children of both sexes within one family unit has proportionately decreased. As a result, the psychology of the tilted child is also becoming more prevalent today.

There are several unique developmental issues that affect tilted families, specifically, the parent's sense of loss or failure about not having children of both sexes; gender or sex-role switching; the physical and emotional isolation of the parent who is not gender paired with any of the children; and problems with autonomy and decision issues between the same-sex children, (similar to the two-child family situation).

In most tilted families, the laterborn children bear the weight of the parent's disappointment and frustration over not having at least one child of the opposite sex. The third or fourth child is often the tilted family's "last hope" for an opposite gender child, and the familiar tilted parental refrain, "Oh no, not another boy (or girl)" may haunt the tilted laterborn for many years. It doesn't take a keen imagination to picture the kinds of acceptance and love issues that such a child could experience. He or she could be the final "disappointment" to the parents and the siblings.

On the flip side, if this third or fourth child is the longed-for opposite sex, he or she may become the favorite and "darling" of the family, at the expense of the two or three older same-sex siblings, who may begin to exhibit symptoms of resentment and hostility towards the family favorite.

Ideally, all parents should look forward to the birth of their children without expectations, however, in reality most parents who do not have children of both sexes somehow feel a sense of loss. The way in which they deal with their disappointment and sense of loss, is, of course, critical to the health and constructive functioning of the family.

An example of positive coping with this tilted family issue is a father of all sons who coaches a girl's softball team, in addition to his activities with his boys. Negatively dealt with, this same father could act out his disappointment and grief by having an extra-marital affair with a young woman who represents the "daughter he always wanted."

The sex-role switching or confusion that often exists in the tilted family may often arise from the parents' unresolved feelings of guilt, loss and inadequacy. In a family of all girls, for instance, one or more of the daughters may take on a masculine role and become the "tomboy" of the family, in order to compensate Daddy for the "son he never had."

In my own experience, I have found that Mars and Venus in dynamic aspect to Saturn and/or Neptune usually appear in the charts of adults who felt devalued by their parents because of their gender. The nodes of the Moon in Cancer/Capricorn, or in the Fourth or Tenth House, may also suggest that a person is especially prone to gender identity problems, such as the ones that appear in tilted families.

To illustrate this scenario more fully, we'll take a case study from my files—"Rachael", a middle-aged woman from a large, conservative midwestern town. Rachael grew up in a two-child, tilted family. She has one sister who is 2 1/2 years her senior. As she remembers it, neither she, nor her sister ever received any real approval from their father. In her words, "He never even told us we were pretty."

True to form, Rachael's tilted father, as the only male family member, expressed his sense of isolation and resentment by suppressing his daughters' feminine identity. Rachael recalled that her father discouraged her and her sister from dating, wearing make-up, buying jewelry, etc. He continually enrolled them in male oriented "confidence building" activities such as karate, and strongly encouraged them in academic subjects such as science and math. Activities and events that encouraged the development and expression of their femininity were systematically eliminated.

Looking at Rachael's chart on the next page, we see that she has Venus and Mars in dynamic aspect to each other, indicating her confusion over her gender identity and role. Her Saturn in the Fifth House squares her Moon (within 2 degrees), which also suggests that Rachael would want to do anything she could in order to gain her father's love and approval, (Fifth House Saturn), even if that meant devaluing and repressing (Saturn) her own femininity (Moon) in order to please him.

Planets in a First Quarter Square to each other often drive

people to actualize and define their own birth identities. Metaphysically speaking, this square may also point to past life identity issues. The element that makes self-identity and individuality such a difficult issue for someone with a First Quarter Square is the person's fear that they will lose their identity if they commit to one specific form of individual expression.

Rachael, rather than assert her own natal and sexual identity needs, gave in to her father's demands that she abstain from sexual relationships as a young and older adult. Interestingly, Rachael's sister became sexually "promiscuous", as a reaction to her father's intense sex "discrimination".

Typical to the tilted family syndrome, Rachael's dynamically aspected Mars and Venus are also in a Disseminating Phase Square. Her Mars/Neptune opposition suggests that she attempted to solve her gender issues by adopting a kind of androgenous identity. This Mars/Neptune opposition also indicates that Rachael was initially the scapegoat (Neptune) for her father's disappointment over never having had a son.

The **applying** Last Quarter Square of a nine degree orb between Mars and Venus also suggests that, metaphysically speaking, this lifetime may be one of Rachael's first exposures to a parentally imposed gender-identity issue. We could say that being born into this tilted-family environment accelerated (Eleventh House) and intensified her process of self-discovery (Mars) in regards to her gender identity (Mars).

As a cautionary note: although, in Rachael's case, the astrological configurations we've discussed in her chart **did** indicate what appears to be a confrontation with her gender identity, we cannot always assume that this is indicated for everyone with the same configurations in their chart.

Again, try to interpret the chart in the **context of the person's family history, birth order, etc.**, rather than from just the configurations themselves. I have found, many times, that younger sibling's charts may indicate a particular issue, as in this case, a tilted-family gender issue. However, because of their birth status, they were seen

RACHAEL'S CHART

Tropical
Placidus
True Node

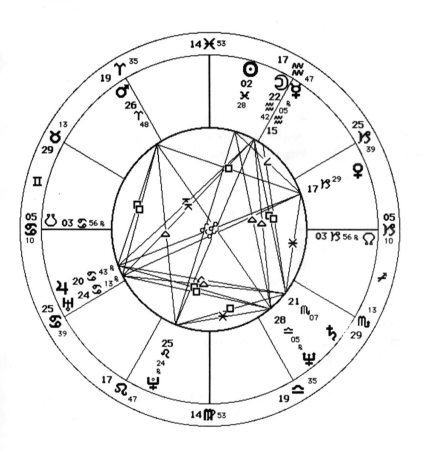

as the baby of the family, and their psychological issues center more around their youngest-child issues, than their tilted family issues.

It's definitely more productive to consider a wide variety of family history, astrological and birth order facts before drawing any conclusions about a person's life issues.

In Rachael's case, her father's projections of his repressed desire for a son, were physically acted out, not so much by Rachael, as by her older sister, even though the sister did **not** have strong gender issue configurations in her chart (other than Saturn square Moon). Yet her behavior more overtly expressed her reaction to her father's sex discrimination than did Rachael's, who had much stronger astrological indications of a gender/identity complex.

This example illustrates the need for interpreting the horoscope in context. Even though Rachael's sister's chart does not overtly indicate an intense gender issue, she was as much or more obviously affected by the tilted-child sex-role confusion than Rachael. So, even though an issue may not appear as a priority in someone's chart, it may be a central life problem that very much needs to be integrated into an astrological counseling session.

It would be an easy mistake for an astrologer to overlook the tilted family issues in Rachael's sister's chart, yet, by "picking up" the Saturn square Moon element, and blending it with her family history, the astrologer could help Rachael's sister to better identify the real issues behind her need to express and assert her femininity in possibly extreme ways.

Another tip in uncovering a tilted family gender role issue is the use of unisex names—Sam for Samantha, Bobby for Roberta, Tony, Lee, Leslie, etc. This is not to say that all those with unisex names are from tilted families, but these names are more frequently used in tilted families.

The tilted family experience can differ widely, depending on the gender-tilting within the family. Male-tilted families appear to have higher levels of sibling disputes and conflict than the female-tilted family groups. Also, significantly higher levels of eating disorders occur in female-tilted families as opposed to male-tilted families.

Female tilting also appears to compromise independent identity growth more than male tilting.

Again, transits of Saturn and/or Neptune to Mars and Venus may bring one or many of these tilted family issues into the foreground of a person's life, sometimes radically and unconsciously effecting a person's self-image, career or relationships during the periods in which they occur.

Astrological counseling, when applied in the context of a person's other life events, can make it easier to move through tough, confrontational astrological periods, although it should never be used in place of clinical or professional help when treating deep psychological and behavioral issues.

The material presented in this book is intended for those who are interested in general self-improvement, self-exploration, or who just want to know more about themselves. So please, use the information only in this light, and seek out professional psychological help and health care treatment when and where it is indicated.

CHAPTER SIX

LARGE FAMILIES

In large families of four or more children, the most important and most emphasized relationships are not those that exist between the parents and children, but rather, those that operate between the siblings in the family.

Because the parents of large families have more demands on their time and energy, there is less one-on-one interaction between them and their individual children, than in families where the parent/child ratio is smaller.

Rules and behavioral guidelines in large families are often developed through basic survival necessities; in other words, a child's family role, personal development and individual needs are more often defined by the needs of the entire family as whole.

This attitude of "working for the good of the whole family" is typical to most large family groups. We could say that larger families, by necessity, emphasize the "collective" consciousness. The children who develop within this environment are more likely to assume collective role identities, as opposed to more sharply defined individual self-identities—especially if the family is dysfunctional.

Working for the benefit of the group may be more of a conscious choice for children of smaller families, but for those from large families, it's usually a matter of necessity. Successful social conformity, cooperation, mutual support and interdependence are the relationship skills that may be dictated and demanded within the large family group. No one in the family has time to "put up" with one member's "eccentricities", or special identity needs, especially if they interrupt or impede general family functioning. Metaphysically speaking, we can speculate that people who are born into large families desire an opportunity through which to learn unique lessons in cooperation, conciliation and mutual interdependence.

In dealing with the horoscopes which I have studied of oldest or older children of large families, I've noticed that their charts frequently show the south node, (which can indicate prior life issues and/or deep security issues), in the sign Libra or the Seventh House, or planets in Libra or the Seventh House.

These configurations suggest that a person's disposition is naturally suited to the older-child role of "head of the family" or family delegator in a large family group. Delegating responsibility and orchestrating smooth and harmonious family functioning tends to be a successful, fulfilling enterprise for people with these astrological configurations.

The south node in Libra or the Seventh House suggests that a person has spent several lives expressing and defining his or her individuality within the group context, and is, perhaps, still overly dependent on the opinions and identity patterns of others (Libra). Having experienced limited opportunity for internal self-definition (north node in Aries or in the First House), people with this birth order position and astrology could benefit from one or more of the identity-defining techniques that are available, provided, of course, that they are not taught within a large group context.

These types of people have probably already learned their group interaction lessons, and so, identity-defining techniques within an "ashram", or religious or metaphysical group setting, (while they appear familiar and appealing), are environments that will offer few new opportunities for individuation to them.

Activities such as meditation, or Tai Chi or other forms of internal self-relation would be indicated here.

If the chart of an older or oldest child of a large family shows the south node in Aries or the First House, or an emphasis of planets in Aries or the First House, the person may well find the birth order role of older child of a large family group almost unbearably constrictive and limiting, and may rebel against it. This person may feel confounded by "fate" or unjustly "imprisoned" within an environment that meets none of his or her identity needs.

However, it's interesting to note that an Aries or First House south node actually equates to a Libra or Seventh House north node, indicating that the present-life lessons (north node) of mutual support and interdependence (Libra/Seventh House) may be a part of this person's life plan, whether their Aries nature likes it or not.

Many people from large families, particularly, "nonconformists" (Aries, Aquarius, etc.), tell me that they are puzzled about the reasons why they were born into such an obviously "inappropriate" and challenging childhood environment. After listening to their stories and examining their charts, I often discover that, while the situation may have seemed obnoxious to them, in actuality, they learned valuable, creative Libran coping skills which in many instances have led to adult career and relationship successes.

Unfortunately, not all "south node in Aries" types are happy about their "enforced" lessons in mutual interdependence. For some, the shock of being born into a large family as the oldest or older child, with all its attendant responsibilities, is so much in opposition to their freedom-loving Aries nature, that it causes intense internal conflict, anger and resentment. Their ardent natal desire for free individual expression is suppressed or ignored by circumstances beyond their control—an extremely difficult situation for a directive, assertive Aries.

In dealing with these types of individuals, I think it's important to emphasize their positive accomplishments as an authority figure within their family, and to discover how the experience may have benefitted their adult lives. Try to avoid the "it was your karmic lesson" approach here, and instead, explore constructive ways in which they can deal with their anger and resentment toward the universe which "randomly" threw them into their intolerable childhood circumstances.

In contrast to the older, south node Aries child, a **younger** or youngest child with south node in Aries or the First House may find that their birth order position blends well with their natural disposition. The youngest child in a large family many times is left free to roam, because the older brothers and sisters have already taken up all the household-chore roles. This is definitely one of the more positive, less challenging developmental contexts, which might suggest that the person is more or less "karmically free", so to speak, to continue to pursue their own Aries needs and desires with a minimum of restrictions or responsibilities.

Because large families tend to be centripetal, (introverted),the planet Mars has special significance for older or oldest siblings of large family groups, especially Mars in the sign Cancer, the Fourth House, or in strong aspect to the Moon. These placements can suggest that there is a conflict between the drive for self-discovery (Mars) and loyalty towards the family (Cancer).

This Mars/Cancer conflict might result in an overly dependent attitude, or lack of commitment to relationships and institutions outside the family.   Again, identity definition and self-relating techniques and activities would be beneficial in this situation.

Younger siblings in large families often experience the collective group experience differently than their elder siblings. Older siblings in large families often feel that they have to act as "buffers" in order to protect their younger brothers and sisters from harmful or damaging dysfunctional parental influences. In the case of alcoholic or workaholic parents, older siblings may act as parental surrogates, nurturing and caring for their younger siblings in place of the psychologically absent or emotionally disturbed parents.

This family situation can promote "survivor guilt" for the elder siblings when they finally leave home. They often feel remorse for "abandoning" their inexperienced younger brothers and sisters to disordered, insecure and chaotic parents. These older siblings may undermine or sabotage their own adult lives and relationships— unconsciously punishing themselves for having left their younger siblings at the mercy of frightening insecurity and confusion in their now virtually parentless home environment.

Older siblings in these circumstances may unconsciously try to "atone" for the "sin" of leaving their younger siblings by choosing a mate or marriage partner whose birth order position is the same as the younger sibling that felt most abandoned when they left home. The mate that the elder sibling chooses as a consequence of their survivor guilt may not be appropriate, having been chosen for an inappropriate reason. Reviewing the relationship dynamics of a person with this profile needs to take this possible survivor guilt attitude into account.

Large families are very often under considerable economic stress. Those with planets in the sign Taurus and the Second House, in particular, may react to this lack of material abundance by becoming single-mindedly obsessed by the acquisition of money and material goods which represent the ultimate form of emotional security and comfort to them.

People with the planet Neptune in the Second House, or the ruler of the Second House aspected to Neptune, on the other hand, may have been conditioned to believe, especially in large families, that material possessions are "bad", or adversely affect spiritual growth. They may feel guilty about having money or material abundance and are often prone to "giving to a fault" in their adult lives.

In both instances, methods that promote positive self-esteem, deservingness, and appreciation of the natural order of abundant living are important issues and attitudes that can benefit these individuals.

A unique birth order position in large families is the solitary gender role—the only boy or girl in a family of four or more children. The blatantly obvious and probably exaggerated parental expectations that can arise from this situation make you feel almost sorry for the child born into this ordinal position.

People in this birth order position will probably learn everything they **never** wanted to know about what their gender role means to their parents. In the horoscope of such an individual, the gendered planets of Mars and Venus, and, (to a lesser extent), their Sun and Moon, in direct aspect to their father's Saturn, (his birth time not required), suggests extreme sensitivity to the father's gender-role expectations, rules, standards, etc.

The dynamics of this single gender, large family birth order position are actually very similar to the solitary sex-role within the tilted family. In both these cases, the single boy or girl may be chosen to fulfill the entire family's implicit or explicit sex-role expectations: the perfect "Barbie" daughter or the macho "Rambo"-type son.

Naturally, people who experience the pressure of this parental or family gender-typing may feel manipulated, controlled, and resentful. In their adult relationships, they may find themselves reacting negatively, consciously or unconsciously, to their friends, mates or co-worker's gender-role expectations or demands: "I'm not going to do all the cooking and cleaning just because I'm a woman".

The primary psychological issue for children of large families seems to be the need to define and express self-identity apart from the group—"I need to find myself, all by myself", as it were. Counseling for children, or adult children of large families certainly needs to emphasize this need for separate identity growth without devaluing the interactive and social skills developed in the large family experience.

Even though identity "lumping" can occur, one of the advantages of large families, whether they are functional or not, is that the siblings frequently form very close, supportive, one-on-one relationships. Often, even into adulthood, these siblings offer each other the unique help, friendship and solace that only a brother or sister, who has known you from your earliest childhood days, can give.

CHAPTER SEVEN

BLENDED FAMILIES

Blended families are the wave of the future. They are currently referred to as the "remarried" family, the "reconstituted" family, the "combination", "bi-nuclear", and "meta-family". Call them what you will, with the divorce rates what they are today, it looks as though the blended family type is here to stay.

Historically, divorce and remarriage were simply not options that were encouraged, or even allowed by civil or religious law for many, many centuries, in previous Eastern and Western cultures. Henry the Eighth had to create a new religion and reshape Western history in order to get his divorce.

The twentieth century, however, has changed all that. Liberal divorce laws and the breakdown of the nuclear family in our country have given rise to the current phenomenon of blended families. Blended or step-families are created when divorced adults remarry and bring their children from their previous marriages into their new marriage, forming a new family group.

The 1980 United States census reported that 1300 step-families were being created **everyday**, and more recent statistics have shown that there are now approximately 25 million step-parents and their 6.5 million children living in blended families. And the complexity of this family configuration is often exaggerated by the fact that more than half of all **second** marriages also end in divorce and subsequent remarriage(s).

Maintaining parental consistency in family rules, behavioral guidelines and lifestyle is extremely difficult even when a family's character and composition remain constant throughout the child raising years. But when the entire family unit experiences one or more spousal changes during the child rearing period, the situation can potentially develop into a nightmare of conflict and emotional turmoil for parents and children alike.

It's only natural that a parent should want to maintain the original family environment in which his or her children have initially been raised. Likewise, their children need and want parental and environmental consistency, and many times, they are resentful and suspicious of a new step-mother or father whose character and expectations may differ radically from the biological or original parent who is being replaced. Add to all of this, the child custody battles that seem to invariably occur when biological or blended families break up, and you have the potential "dynamite" that can produce troubled, psychologically fragmented, socially maladjusted children and young adults.

Probably the most difficult and central issue involved in the blended family situation is the question of loyalty. To which parent or parents do the children most owe their loyalty—to the displaced biological parent, to the new step-parent, or to caring step-parents from previous marriages? Step-children living in blended families usually side with their biological parent during spousal disagreements, or they may polarize to the displaced biological parent or a former step-parent and turn against both parents in their new blended family.

Step-sibling relationships can pose another serious problem for remarried families, because of the feelings of confusion and abandonment for the children involved in the remarriage: "You love your new family more than you love us—you're always on their side", or "Why don't you love Mommy (or Daddy) and me anymore?" Stepchildren will frequently attempt, either deliberately or unconsciously to subvert the new marriage in hopes of reuniting their "real" parents.

The natural parents in these circumstances often feel extreme guilt and remorse that is instigated by their children's grief, insecurity or anger about the new remarried family environment. These internal parental conflicts can be an additional source of stress and upheaval in the family blending process. In considering all of the obstacles to happy blended family functioning, it probably comes as no surprise that current statistics indicate that over 50% of all remarriages end in divorce. Whatever the circumstances, children from broken homes usually face extremely trying and difficult adjustment issues that may seriously affect both their childhood and adult functioning and their outlook on life, relationships, etc.

The step-family has a host of issues and dynamics working against it that the "nuclear" family does not. Within the new step-family, roles and relationships may be undefined; family rules and boundaries are sometimes blurred or unfamiliar, and parental authority issues may be confused, ("Which one of them is running this family, anyway?"). Birth order roles are also frequently compromised when two different families are combined. Sibling birth positions and age-spacing can be changed or duplicated, often confusing the children's family roles and identities.

For example, a step-family has recently been formed, consisting of a father with two daughters (ages 16 and 10) and a mother of two sons, (age 15 and 12). The biggest birth order conflict that could arise here is between the oldest daughter (16) of the father, and the eldest son (15) of the mother, neither of which is going to want to relinquish their authority status as the remarried family's eldest sibling.

One advantage in this situation is that the eldest siblings are of the opposite sex, so each will retain their individual gender role identities in the new family (oldest boy, eldest girl). However, if the eldest children were both male in this situation, the effect on the family's functioning could be disastrous. Same-sex, same-age step-siblings can cause one of the most bitter and destructive dynamics that occur in remarried families, especially if these two step-siblings are teenagers.

In our hypothetical family, if the father's eldest child of 16 were male, rather than female, the 15 year-old mother's son would now be "sandwiched" between his 16 year-old stepbrother and his own 12 year old biological brother. This eliminates his original birth order role as the eldest child and oldest brother of his first family, and places him in a new role as the second male child and one of three brothers in the remarried family. From this 15 year-old teenager's point of view, the new step-family is a total "bust." He feels displaced and is angry, bitter and resentful towards his step-siblings, his step-father and his biological mother who has "betrayed" him by forcing him into an "inferior" and entirely unfamiliar birth order role.

This adolescent may attempt to assert his natal eldest-brother role overtly, through direct conflict and fighting with his step-brother, or, perhaps, subliminally, by trying to undermine his step-brother's relationship to his natural father by vying for his affection in order to usurp the stepbrother's new status as oldest, and most favored male in the new step-family.

While the two oldest males are battling for dominance in the new family, the new step-mother and her step-daughter, in contrast, are enjoying their relationship as the only females of the family. However, this new alliance does not bode well for the mother's youngest son, because his favored youngest-child, "Mama's little boy" status now feels threatened by his mother's intimacy and closeness with her new step-daughter.

During step-family parental disagreements, and particularly during spousal arguments over how to discipline the children, step-siblings usually line up biologically on either side of the issue— the "blood is thicker than water" psychology. The most familiar phrase that arises in these situations usually comes from the step-children: "You can't tell me what to do—you're not my mother (or father)".

An often unavoidable and unfortunate effect of authority conflicts in step-families is that the children can end up wielding tremendous power over their parents and family functioning as a whole—far beyond what influence they would possess in a nuclear family where the parental authority roles and boundaries are more likely to be clearly defined, acknowledged and accepted. Children in remarried families may try to emotionally blackmail their natural parents by laying on "guilt trips" that often make the parents cave-in to their every childish demand: "If you hadn't left Mommy, and married this other woman, I wouldn't be so miserable—so you owe me."

Psychologists have noted that children who lose their biological mother through death or remarriage appear to have more emotional conflicts and disturbances than those who lose their fathers through death or divorce. Children who remain with their biological mother or central mother figure through a divorce, and her remarriage, appear to suffer less from anxiety and conflict in the step-family situation and feel less threatened by abandonment and acceptance issues than do those who have lost their mother in the divorce process.

The natal sense of security, intense caring, nurturing and love, seems to be universally perceived by children as generating primarily from the birth mother or mother figure. In folklore and fairytales, for example, remarriage always seems to result in a Cinderella, Snow White or Hansel and Gretel-style wicked stepmother.

In continuing our study on the blended family psychology, we'll examine a case study of a woman, "Lisa", whose natural mother and father divorced when she was nine years old. A year after the divorce, her mother remarried a divorced man and Lisa and her younger sister (6 years old), went with their mother to live with the new stepfather. Lisa's stepfather had a son (10) and a daughter (8) of his own, however, they lived with own mother after the divorce, and visited their father and his new family only on weekends.

Lisa, as the firstborn daughter of a tilted (same gender) family, was very close to her biological father. She admitted that she still holds a grudge against her father for "deserting" her in the divorce. Her father had represented a positive and caring opposite-gender role model in her life for nine years, and losing him in the divorce was a severe blow—(the loss of a father is usually most damaging to the firstborn child). Firstborns often react to the loss of their father by trying to "fill his shoes"—becoming super-responsible or overachieving perfectionists, or by turning their anger and rage toward society in general—"Everything is in life is so unfair."

A first glance at Lisa's chart reveals a Tenth House emphasis and a Capricorn Moon. Both these factors suggest that she would be receptive to adopting the role as the stabilizer in her natal family. Because of her tendency to over-identify with her parents, and in particular, her father's, marital conflicts, Lisa tried to compensate for her parents' relationship problems by taking on the role of surrogate wife to her father. After her parent's divorce, Lisa lost her coveted role as her father's "best girl" and surrogate wife, and from that point on, Lisa felt as though her emotional and social life became, in her words, "suppressed and stunted behind a bulwark of rock."

Having lost her role as "wife" to her father, and unable to transfer it to her aloof step-father, Lisa moved on to the next available male, her step-brother, for the fulfillment of the physical closeness she had shared with their father. At one point, Lisa physically displaced her intense need for male intimacy onto her step-brother by initiating sexual advances and contact with him, which, when discovered by her mother and step-father, almost destroyed the marriage.

In reality, attitudes of hostility or indifference between step-siblings may often mask their inner conflicts over deep, unacknowledged emotions of sexual attraction. Sibling rivalry is one thing for parents to handle; sexual attraction between step-siblings is another. Most parents of blended families are unprepared for sexual feelings between step-siblings, and many find this situation particularly threatening.

However, when children in blended families are unable to duplicate or acquire in their step-families, the same parental love relationships that they shared in their original families, their unmet emotional needs may be transferred to their step-siblings in the inappropriate form of sexual interaction.

In Lisa's case, her sexual advances towards her step-brother may have had two motives, the first one being her desire to duplicate her relationship with her biological father and, also her need to find a way of getting back at her mother for having driven away her beloved father.

Although father-daughter sexual abuse cases are now rampant, recent studies have shown that sexual interaction between siblings occurs **five times** as often as between fathers and daughters, probably because there is much less social awareness and no civil laws regarding sibling incest.

In looking at Lisa's chart, (next page), we see a Capricorn Moon, suggesting that it was "easy" for her to attempt to duplicate or transfer her surrogate wife family role. The emphasis on the Earth element in

LISA'S CHART

Tropical
Placidus
True Node

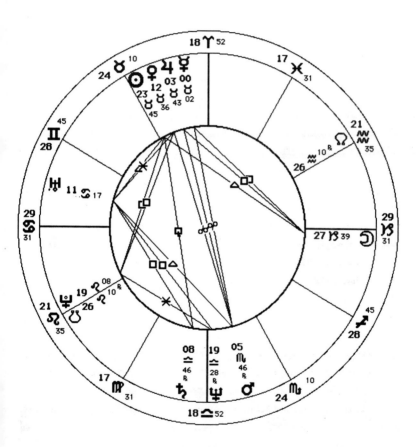

her chart also indicates that her physical contact and closeness to her biological father, or some male figure, was a much needed factor in her life.

Lisa's Fourth House Mars in Scorpio, **retrograde**, opposing her Mercury, Jupiter and Venus in Taurus suggests that her displaced anger, (Mars), over her parents' divorce expressed itself as sexual attraction (Mars again) toward her stepbrother. It also indicates that Lisa was unconsciously attracted to sexual (Mars) taboos (Scorpio) and felt compelled (Scorpio) to break the family (Fourth House) and societal (Fourth House/Tenth House) sexual taboo of sibling incest.

Saturn, Neptune and Mars retrograde gathered around her Ic, are also indications of repeated lifetime experiences of separation, betrayal and loss of family support (Scorpio), which provoked vindictiveness (Scorpio) and anger (Mars) towards those responsible for her suffering.

Mars in the Fourth House opposing Mercury, (ruler of the Third), is a clear indication of the possibility of sexual activity in the home with a step-brother. People with Mars retrograde, need to utilize their sexual energy in ways that promote spiritual growth, rather than as a means of expressing poorly channeled, unresolved, anger or power issues, such as we see in Lisa's case.

The Mars aspect of loyalty to one's own identity development also comes into play in Lisa's chart. Her adolescence occurred shortly after her entrance into her blended family, at which point she began striving for more character definition, sexual identity and independence (Mars), but because of her particular problems, her sexual drive was inappropriately expressed inside, rather than outside the family unit.

Lisa's sexual issues, and those of many teenagers in new blended families, are confused, many times, by the overt expression of sexuality between the step-parents whose romantic passions have not yet "cooled" when their children enter adolescence. In the nuclear family, most parents' romantic ardor is less overtly expressed by the time their children reach puberty, and they often represent less confusing sexual role models to their children.

Lisa had been through a considerable amount of therapy before coming for astrological counseling, and was, therefore, quite open to accepting and working with the issues that were raised in reviewing her astrology. I suggested that the upcoming transit of Saturn, (father), to her Seventh House Capricorn Moon, would present an excellent opportunity for her to resolve her grief over the loss of her father, (Saturn/Capricorn), and better understand the way in which her loss was manifested as sexual impulses towards her stepbrother.

We also discussed her tendency to project her Capricorn Moon into her romantic relationships, which expressed itself as her desire for strong, stable fatherly men, and I suggested that she find a safe, therapeutic environment in which to work through residual anger, depression and grief over the loss of her father.

Lisa said that she had benefitted from therapeutic body-work techniques, particularly the Reichian method, which helped her to release her "stuffed" emotions and "body armor" (Tenth House) that she had developed in trying to cope with her parent's divorce and her step-family life.

The problems and issues that face the blended family are truly above and beyond the capacity of many parents to deal with and solve. Loyalty issues, changed and disordered birth order roles, identity confusion, poorly defined or distorted authority and power positions—all are potent, difficult issues in their own right, but combined, can become an impossible "powder keg" of disruption when poorly handled within the remarried family.

Because step-families are a rapidly growing social phenomenon, blended family parents need to educate themselves in the art of step-family survival. The sheer number and weight of the extra challenges facing remarried families is almost staggering when studied objectively.

I personally feel that the "what the hell, let's go for it" attitude of uninformed and overexcited divorced couples who decide to 'take the plunge', without seriously considering the **real** impact of remarriage on their children, is naive and potentially very dangerous and destructive for their children and themselves.

Successful remarriage with children requires a great deal of forethought and knowledge. Fortunately, there are many effective forms of family counseling that, when used and integrated, can be strong, "preventive medicine" for the health and survival of the blended family.

Recently formed step-families can also benefit from a thorough examination of family members' birth order roles and individual astrological affinities. So much confusion, bad feeling and conflict can be circumvented when families are aware of their individual natal identity and birth order differences and needs. Integrating this awareness into the blended family environment could contribute immensely to preventing psychological damage or divorce for newly blended step-family members.

CHAPTER EIGHT

"SPECIAL" FAMILIES

There are a number of special family circumstances that change or modify the way in which a family functions and inter-relates. Infant or child deaths in the family, (including miscarriages and stillbirths), children with disabilities, adoptions and gifted children are the exceptional circumstances that we'll be exploring in this chapter.

Death of a child: The death of a child always changes the sibling order and structure of a family, and is therefore, even aside from the intense emotions of loss and grief, extremely disruptive to family functioning. Probably the most difficult and crucial step for the family, following such a loss, is the letting go of the deceased infant or child and the completion of the grieving process.

Suppressed or hidden emotions of grief, anger or "holding on" in the parents can have dire consequences for their other children. Parents in these situations very often will fall into "if only" scenarios, or may elevate the deceased child to the position of "dead hero" or idol, to whom none of the other children compare. They might also unconsciously choose one of their children to take the vacated birth role of their deceased brother or sister.

Any or all of these parental attitudes can be devastating to the surviving siblings, who may feel lost, bewildered, displaced or devalued as a result of their parent(s)' inappropriate reactions to their child's death.

As an example, the loss of a dearly loved and valued firstborn teenage son devastates his parents so completely that they lose interest in and devalue their secondborn daughter. The daughter, depressed and burdened by her parents' apathy, grows up with an extremely poor self-image. She feels inherently worthless and inadequate and also experiences stubborn and chronic illnesses, particularly female "complaints", that do not respond to traditional medical treatment, probably because they have their source in her own unresolved internal gender struggle, i.e., her conflict in appreciating and valuing her femininity which her parents devalued because of the unresolved trauma of their only son's death.

Additionally, this daughter, after her brother's death, stepped into the role as the oldest and only child in the family, and she took on the responsibilities and issues of these other birth order positions in place of her own natural second-child, younger-sister- of-a-brother family role. In almost all cases, children who step into a vacated sibling role after the death of their brother or sister, will feel devalued, displaced and not appreciated for who they really are by parents and other family members.

Miscarriages are not technically included under the category of infant mortality, however, they can be just as devastating as the death of an infant or older child, especially if they occur later in the pregnancy when the parents and family have already given the child a name, its own room, playthings, a crib, etc.

The more advanced the pregnancy, the greater the loss of the baby through miscarriage is felt by the parents and siblings. As in all other cases of sibling death in the family, the surviving siblings may unconsciously experience survivor guilt and be obsessed throughout their lives by feelings that they somehow have no right to their lives, because their deceased sibling was deprived of his or her life.

Also, if a child is born soon after the miscarriage they may be "haunted" by the feeling that they should have been someone else, that they are only a replacement for some other unknown child, (the unknown "other" being, of course, their deceased sibling). These "ghosts" in "replacement" childrens' pasts needs to be consciously recognized and "exorcised" in order for them to get on with their own lives and to experience joy and fulfillment in their own identity. Psychodrama or personality integration therapies are often beneficial in these cases.

In astrology, new beginnings are symbolized by the person's ascendant. How the person instinctively approaches new life experiences is indicated by the sign rising on the horizon (the ascending sign) which is present at the time of birth. The ascendant acts as the lens through which we perceive and judge the world in which we function; our perception's, values, beliefs and self-image, as well as the tone or quality of our family environment are all involved with or symbolically represented by the ascendant in our charts.

In relation to sibling deaths, in my experience, if the ascending sign is Aquarius, or if the ruler of the ascendant is positioned in the Eleventh House or is in the sign Aquarius, or if the planet Uranus is conjoined the ascendant, the person may, in fact, be acting out the role as the replacement child for his dead brother or sister. Again, caution in counseling is indicated here, because these interpretations need to be given in the context of the whole person.

One of the strongest indicators that the replacement child psychology may be operating in the person's life is an intense feeling of insecurity and fear that they cannot fit in, or become an integral, important part of any career or social grouping. Feelings of rejection, low-self esteem and ambivalence about purpose and place in life are also indications that their Aquarius rising, their ruler of the ascendant in the Eleventh House or in the sign Aquarius or Uranus on the ascendant are referring to an unresolved sibling death and its related impact on them.

Parents who lose a child when the planets Uranus, Neptune or Pluto (especially the latter two) are in dynamic aspect to their Moon, may experience accentuated difficulty in successfully coming to terms with their grief, loss and anguish. This is because the child's death within this astrological context can symbolically represent the realization of the parent's worst fears—the irretrievable loss of their child (Moon). Uranus, Neptune and Pluto are transpersonal planets, and when in aspect to the Moon, may produce those dreaded, seemingly vindictive, uncontrollable "acts of fate" that can insensibly and irrevocably snatch vulnerable little children from their parents' loving and protective arms.

The loss of a child during these astrological periods may "cut to the core" of the parents' being—the meaning and purpose of their love, marriage, family, etc. seem somehow hopelessly doomed to failure. Child deaths during these cycles can require even greater effort and support on the part of the parents, family members, friends and relatives in order to successfully cope with and complete the grieving process, so that the family as a whole can continue to successfully grow and function.

Stillbirths can also leave parents with deep emotional scars, pervasive guilt or deep feelings of inadequacy. Approximately one out of every 100 infants are stillborn, often for reasons beyond the reach of current medical knowledge. By definition a baby is stillborn if it dies somewhere in the time between the twentieth week of pregnancy and birth. At this time, the baby is fully formed and recognizable; the expectant parents have probably successfully endured the trials of many months of pregnancy, and so experience enormous trauma and pain when the baby is suddenly, and many times, inexplicably, lost. Blame, thoughts of suicide, battles with in-laws, or drug and alcohol use are often consequences of poorly handled emotions of grief and anguish over the loss of an infant, and at this time, the family must find access through counseling and group help to the support, love and caring that will heal and reconnect their family circle.

In contrast to infant sibling deaths, the death of an older child or adolescent in a family, causes the entire family hierarchy or sibling role structure to shift. Whereas the death of the youngest child may be most traumatic for the parents, the death of oldest or middle children severely disrupts sibling relationships and family functioning as a whole, for the obvious reason that the infant death does not have the same "ripple effect" of shifting all the birth order roles in the family, as does the death of an already established, role-playing elder child.

Although an elder sibling death dramatically affects the family as a whole, the deceased child's next younger sibling is likely to be the person most affected. In a three-child family, for example, the death of the secondborn or middlechild does not affect the birth order role of the oldest firstborn child. However, with the death of the second sibling, the thirdborn or youngest child becomes the secondchild, rather than the third, and his or her entire family orientation and birth order role changes. Again, it is extremely important that these birth order role shifts be acknowledged and properly handled.

Issues of death in the family are so traumatic and the grieving process is so deep and difficult that I never attempt to deal with these areas on my own. When these issues come up during astrological counseling, I invariably direct the person to professional counselors who specifically deal with death, loss, and grieving therapies.

Disabilities: Mentally retarded or physically disabled siblings present another difficult challenge to successful family functioning. Through guilt or imitation, "normal" siblings often identify with their disabled sister or brother and may act out their disabled siblings physical or psychological behavior and characteristics. The normal siblings may also feel the need to compensate for their "damaged" public family image by striving for social acceptance or popularity with their peers, or by hiding or lying about their "awful" family secret. Unfortunately, the guilt that can arise from upholding the family image at the expense of the handicapped sibling may result in feelings on the part of the normal siblings of self-disgust and self-hatred, which may manifest later in life as drug addiction, failed careers and relationship problems.

Blame is also a big issue in the case of handicapped children. Everyone in the family has a theory about who was responsible for the handicap, and a great deal of family time and energy may be devoted to finding a scapegoat for the "accident". The emotionally charged atmosphere that such blame and finger-pointing creates invariably leads to unhappy, seriously disturbed family functioning. Children who come from this type of family background may grow into guilt-ridden, confused adults who externally project their inner conflicts by blaming and attacking others.

People who mirror a retarded sibling's character traits in their own behavior will frequently show strong connections or aspects from other planets to Neptune. Learned helplessness, continual "spacing-out", or problems relating to the external world also point to the possibility that a sibling may be unconsciously **imitating** or identifying with his retarded brother or sister. Drug-addiction and substance abuse (Neptune/Pisces/Twelfth House) may have their roots here as well.

Those with an emphasized Sixth House or planets in Virgo may become workaholics or underachievers in response to their internalized guilt feelings about their retarded or handicapped sibling's "misfortune".

Adoption: A child adopted at birth or shortly thereafter fits into the adoptive family's birth order structure in the same way that the parents' own biological infant would be integrated. However, if the adopted child is older and has already developed role patterns and behavioral characteristics in another family or institutional setting, the impact of the adoption on the adoptive family is much greater, and may lead to adjustment problems for the whole family. In these cases, additional parental time, patience and attention is required in order to blend the adopted child into the already established family "pecking order".

In general, integrating adopted children into the family is less stressful and challenging than bringing together stepchildren and step-parents in the blended family, because the adoptive family siblings are usually given a voice in the decision to bring another child into the family. The event is usually well thought out, planned and anticipated by all the existing family members, whereas, in divorce situations, new step-families are often created without the approval or consent of the children, and the adjustment process may be accompanied by much more resentment and resistance than in the case of an adoption.

This is not to say that all adoptions are successful. Many adopted children become over-achievers in their attempts to fit in and "prove themselves" to the adoptive family, or, conversely they may develop into underachievers as result of their feelings of not being wanted or loved by their adoptive parents and siblings.

In working with adults who were adopted as children, I have noticed that Moon outer-contact planets, such as Moon/Uranus, Moon/Neptune or Moon/Pluto commonly appear in their charts. Periods of contact to these points in an adopted adult's horoscope signal excellent opportunities in which to review the past —perhaps to discover who the biological parents were and why they decided to give their child up for adoption. It is also common for these contact periods to bring up issues of abandonment and rejection, so that they can be recognized and hopefully resolved.

Families with Gifted Children: Giftedness in this context refers to more than the intelligence quotient determined by standardized tests. Unusually high levels of task commitment and creativity are also considered as "gifted" attributes.

Unlike a death or disability in the family, which has an immediate impact, siblings of gifted children usually do not manifest reactions to their gifted siblings differences for at least five years from the time that the child has been notably "labeled" or determined to be gifted.

Also, if the parents of a gifted child are not emotionally or developmentally receptive to the child's special needs, the child can become conflicted about his or her talents and may try to hide or deny his differences from his parents, teachers, friends and siblings. By repressing their abilities, gifted children often evade their guilt about being "better" than other children, and reduce the risk of social alienation by not expressing their true abilities.

If the gifted child's parents are over-achievers themselves, they may fail to notice their gifted child's special talents because their parental expectations are already so overinflated. On the other hand, parents who feel a sense of inadequacy about their own talents, could be threatened by their child's remarkable abilities and may try to ignore or discourage the child's self-expression and achievements.

Very much like families with a retarded or disabled child, family members of gifted children who do not own up to their latent hostility or resentment towards the "special" child can end up treating the gifted sibling as the family scapegoat. Adult gifted children with this background often find it difficult to escape their childhood "stigma" and may have to struggle to maintain any type of appropriate career or life work. Or, they may reach a plateau of professional success but still wrestle with their feelings of inferiority and lack of self-esteem.

I have seen a number of gifted children's horoscopes, however, I have not noted any consistent commonalities among them, and do not support the idea of a "cookbook" signature by which a gifted child can be identified.   I generally begin with an examination of the person's birth order and family structure and explore their gifted issue in the light of the entire family history.

For example, in the case of an eldest gifted child, the parents may have overinflated or rigid performance expectations which arise more from the fact that the child is their firstborn, than from their perceptions of his or her special abilities.   In this case, the person would be dealing within their firstborn birth order issues, as well as their gifted issue.

In another scenario, the gifted abilities of a middle or laterborn child in a large family (4 or more children), may be completely overlooked, not because his or her talents are not obvious to other family members, but simply because of the difficult logistics involved in meeting the needs of one special child, when there are so many siblings clamoring for attention. Here, again, the gifted issue is combined with large-family identity issues.

Another situation that can evolve in the case of a gifted child, is the bond that sometimes develops between the child and his or her "adoring" mother. In this case, the mother may give the child verbal or unconscious messages that their "extraordinary" talents put them on a "higher", inaccessible level in relation to their peers, and that only she, the mother, can really understand and provide what her "special" child requires in life. Naturally, this dynamic increases the child's sense of alienation and separation from peers and people in general.

A gifted **youngest** child is many times seen as a challenge to the authority of the family's sibling hierarchy. The older children in the family may be threatened by the child's accelerated learning abilities and may resent any extra attention that the child receives from parents, teachers, etc. Deep sibling rivalry issues may result, and feelings of hatred could be aimed at the youngest gifted child. The parents, in an attempt to relieve the offending sibling "inequities" in the home, may aggressively discourage and repress the gifted child's expression of his or her special talents, so as to restore sibling harmony.

Deep depression, feelings of inadequacy, self-doubt or feelings of intimidation are the most common legacy of abuse of the gifted child. Group therapies that foster self-esteem, social integration and identity definition can be beneficial to gifted children or adults, who need to explore methods of meaningfully integrating their special talents into a creative school, career and lifestyle setting that is fulfilling to them and beneficial to the society in which they function. It is important for gifted people to realize that, regardless of their family backgrounds, they can make needed and valued contributions to their society and the world.

In all, special families have special needs, and children who grow up with any of these exceptional family circumstances will require constructive, consistent, parental or professional guidance and counseling. Astrological counseling, also, can offer several insights that may increase a person's awareness of the dynamics that are or were at work in their "exceptional" family and may lead to other forms of self-improvement work and therapy as well.

PART THREE

THE MAJOR BIRTH ORDER POSITIONS

CHAPTER NINE

THE FIRSTBORN OR OLDEST CHILD

The category of firstborn or eldest children is the largest birth order position group, and comprises a larger segment of the U.S. population than any of the other birth positions.

As the first, and for a time, only child enters their lives, parents are likely to feel that this, their first baby, holds special value and meaning for them. A panoply of unique parental emotions accompanies the birth of the first child. Intense excitement, pride, and anticipation, as well as fear, insecurity and anxiety arise as this huge, and many times completely new and unfamiliar responsibility suddenly drops out of "nowhere". Parents usually undergo a good deal of psychological and physical preparation during pregnancy, however, the reality of the first birth is usually an adjustment "jolt" for which no first-time mother or father is ever truly prepared.

First-child jitters are common to new mothers and fathers, and often result in the parents' "eggshell" attitude towards their new baby: "Am I doing this right? I'm afraid I might hurt her; what do we do now?" For the majority of new parents, the firstborn phenomenon triggers a host of doubts and insecurities about how to raise their new child—"Why don't they come with an instruction manual?", is probably the most common psychological reaction.

For all these reasons, the firstborn is subjected to an entirely different family atmosphere than their succeeding siblings. Because they're first, firstborns are usually the unintentional "guinea pigs" of parental experimentation. Many parents see their firstborn child as the fulfillment of all their hopes and dreams, and in many cases, they have the child's entire life planned, even before the birth. The unrealistically high expectations that are often placed on firstborns by their parents are usually a result of this parental "firstborn" psychology: "Our child will have everything we never had and will have all the opportunities that were denied to us."

Historically, firstborn or eldest children have symbolized the secured continuance of a specific family line, a tribe, clan, or even country. The highest hopes and expectations of their parents, clansmen or countrymen could be placed on a firstborn's shoulders from the moment of birth—not an easy role to fulfill.

From antiquity, firstborns, especially males, have been the "defenders of the faith" for their families and have been given the responsibility for upholding and carrying on social traditions and structures. For many cultures, they have symbolized the "passing of the torch" from one generation to another—they nurture and protect their family and cultural traditions from the onslaught of new, "subversive" ideas and events.

As the symbolic generational "bridge", firstborns, even in modern times, may act out their archetypal role by blocking progressive, new ideas from entering their family or society— maintaining the status-quo. Or, conversely, they may attempt to blend past and present beliefs into greater or more evolved, new traditions. In reality, though, the oldest child usually does block, rather than champion new ideas or progressive thinking.

Although the significance of the firstborn may no longer be what it was historically, (probably as a result of the burgeoning world population, sweeping societal changes, and the breakdown of the traditional family structure), it still holds special challenges for the child and parents. Lucille Forer, a family psychologist, in her book, **Birth Order and Life Roles**, discusses the potential challenges of the firstborn birth position: "In effect, the first child often becomes a 'laboratory experiment' in which the parents must invent new behavior, experience new feelings and rely on minimal prior learning vis-a-vis their new offspring...first children are the sole recipient of all the loving, well-meaning attention of the parents—and also the sole recipient of their pressures, worries and admonitions, too."

In Roman mythology, the god Janus (January) had two faces, one, old and bearded, the other, youthful and full of hope. This two-faced god can be seen as symbolizing the firstborn's conflicting "faces"—the one which looks back, oversees and maintains the traditions of the past, or of the father (Saturn), and the other face of the son (Jupiter) which looks forward to a new future. In Roman mythology, the god Saturn (representing time and tradition), is overthrown by his son, Jupiter, (representing the new present and future), and imprisoned in Hades—Pluto's, (brother of Jupiter) domain, (a great brother to have around!).

Firstborns who have Jupiter and Saturn in direct aspect often are unconsciously enmeshed in this mighty historical, archetypal battle for dominance between the old (tradition) and the new (the future). I usually suggest some type of Jungian psychotherapy for firstborns, because Jung's work with deals specifically with archetypal figures in the unconscious. Jung's work has led to a much greater awareness and conscious communication with these extremely powerful and often conflicted sub-personalities, who can, especially in the case of firstborns, make life seem more like a battleground than a fulfilling learning experience.

The family history of one client of mine in particular, "Rich", vividly illustrates this "classic" firstborn-son dilemma. Rich was born into a wealthy, upper class, centrifugal (extraverted) family. His father was, predictably, extremely extraverted, status conscious, and a firstborn son himself. His mother was a secondborn of two sisters, and was content with her position as the subdominant parent. Rich also had two younger sisters.

In Rich's own words, he was "born and bred to be the ideal son in the American tradition". His role in the family amounted to that of the family "prince" and heir, to whom all parental favors and opportunities were offered. As in most strictly patriarchal family structures, Rich, as the firstborn male, was lavished with privileges and family resources that were almost entirely denied to his two younger sisters. Rich's family situation was an extreme, blatant example of parental gender favoritism. Both his parents supported the patriarchal family myth about the inherent worthlessness of female offspring. Rich stated that his father overtly deprived his sisters of time, money and opportunities in order to focus all the family resources on him—the "heir to the throne".

In terms of traditional family sex roles, Rich's family actually functioned quite smoothly—the firstborn male family hierarchy (Rich and his father) controlling the submissive, subjugated female family contingency "led" by the sub-dominant secondborn mother.

Rich's chart (next page), shows a Leo rising sign, which indicates his natural inclination and desire to imitate and please his ambitious, egocentric father. Throughout his childhood, Rich got good grades in school, joined the "right" clubs, socialized with the "correct" people, and in general carried on his family image and legacy.

However, as he moved into adulthood, Rich's doubts and uneasiness about his patriarchal favored-son role surfaced. He began to question his father's beliefs and values and to psychologically distance himself from his father's influence. His Saturn and Pluto in Leo in the First House suggest that Rich had a need to actualize a **total** transformation of his own inner father image and to establish his own inner authority and standards apart from those of his biological father.

This inner dichotomy created guilt feelings in Rich about rejecting his father's favoritism (Saturn/Pluto conflict). Also, his Saturn in the First House contributed to his insecurity and grieving about the loss or "death" (Pluto) of his traditional father image (Saturn). Rich's sense of loss and mourning was again compounded by his firstborn status, because firstborns have intense parental loyalty issues—they often feel remorseful and guilty about not living up to even ridiculously high performance standards set up by their fathers.

Looking at his chart from a metaphysical point of view, Rich's south node in Sagittarius in the Fifth House (exactly trine his Leo sun), and the ruler Jupiter in Scorpio in the Fourth House, suggest prior life patterns of acting out the role of the child prodigy who is raised by a famous, ambitious, powerful father figure. Jupiter is also in a First Quarter Square to his First House Saturn and Pluto, suggesting extreme emotional pressure (square) from a family member (his father), to conform (Saturn).

RICH'S CHART

Tropical
Placidus
True Node

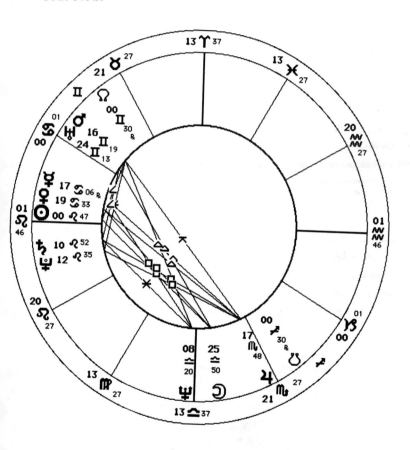

His Saturn/Jupiter First Quarter Square, on the other hand, indicates Rich's need to form his own identity and reality apart from his father's. This situation can, of course, call for great courage in "going against the tide" of family and parental influence. It can also bring up the firstborn's feeling that it might be better "all around" to suffer the internal pain of repressing one's own inner identity needs rather than to risk personal and worldly "failure" as a result of rebelling against the establishment. Spiritually speaking, it is the effort towards achieving independence, more than the result, that is important here.

Rich's natal Mars in Gemini, ruling his Tenth House conjoined Uranus does **not** suggest a strong inner pull or desire to conform to his family's traditions (Tenth House). In fact, it is more suggestive of a family rebel who refuses to relate to the family past.

The ruler of his north node Mercury, in Cancer in his Twelfth House, suggests that his life "mission" is to completely retreat (Twelfth House) from the external world and its values, and to subsequently develop his own inner security (Cancer), apart from any parental or social expectations. This configuration also indicates that Rich "sees" a vision of a new future for the world, and that his knowledge and education (Gemini) are to be used for the benefit of the whole of humanity (Eleventh House), rather than for the benefit of one person (Fifth House) or group of people (his family).

This father/son conflict created a crisis in Rich's psyche and outer life, illustrated by his Mars inconjunct his Jupiter. Rich discussed the fact that he had often felt that he would lose his mind in trying to walk the tightrope between his own and his father's desires. Rich's mental "fragmentation" (Eleventh House Mars), and his admitted lack of concentration (Mercury retrograde in the Twelfth House), resulted from his struggle with and resistance to his own inner voice. His Twelfth House Sun is semi-square his Mars and sesqui-square his Jupiter, which is an added indication of Rich's ambivalent (Twelfth House) attitude about the real nature of his life purpose (Sun). However, his First House Saturn/Jupiter square suggests that as he continues to make repeated efforts to define his true life purpose, that it will be revealed to him.

Rich's Fourth House Libra Moon indicates that he also played the role of family peacemaker (Chapter Two), which makes it all the more the difficult, as he said, to "throw a wrench" into his father's dreams and aspirations for his only son—the heir and future head of the family. He admitted that his adult drive for self-identity had created a very negative relationship between his father and himself.

When Rich came to see me, he was very involved in the environmental protection politics, and in disseminating information on new technologies, which satisfies his Saturn/Pluto conjunction (breaking away from the old order) and his north node, Mars, and Uranus in his Eleventh House (revolutionary, innovative ideas). At the time of our first meeting (January 1990), transit Saturn was in his Sixth House squaring his Moon.

I suggested to him that this transit presented an excellent opportunity for discovering and exploring his paternal patterning and the self-critical, self-doubting, unworthiness attitudes that his father/son conflicts had created in his psyche. I also suggested that his workaholic tendencies (Sixth House) could be dealt with by under-standing and releasing the negative overachieving aspect of his firstborn birth order position. Saturn was opposing his Venus in Cancer at this time, and I pointed out that this would also be a good time to resolve his self-esteem issues; in other words, Rich needed to overcome his belief that his value as a person could only be measured by what he externally accomplished in life.

In forecasting ahead, Saturn opposing itself and his natal Pluto in 1992 indicated that he would begin to concretely realize the fruits of his self-definition and self-improvement work. Saturn above the horizon suggest a "coming-out" period for Rich, during which he would feel more valued and self-defined in his own right, as compared (Seventh House) to feeling identified with his father's character and values. I mentioned also, that he would probably benefit greatly from rolfing or rebirthing therapies which would assist him in physically expressing and releasing his anger and resentment towards his father.

Expectations placed on firstborns may seem like natural and

necessary motivational psychology to the parents, however, the child may come to view them quite differently. In the case of a 40 year-old firstborn woman, "Mary", who came to me for astrological counseling, her parents' expectations seemed more like a noose around her neck than loving parental guidelines or inspiration.

Mary's parents were an oldest-child mother and only-child father. Both had college degrees in business, and would, ideally, have preferred a "strong", pragmatic firstborn son who was interested in academics and business, and who would be a credit to his parents' (especially the father's) personal, social and career "successes"—three strikes against Mary.

Mary, contrary to her parent's expectations and hopes, was a female firstborn, who evinced interest, not in academics, business, or worldly success, but in art, of all things—ceramics, painting and drawing—"unproductive" activities that were a blatant "waste of time" in her parents' opinion. Had her mother and father been second or third children themselves, they might have been more tolerant of Mary's need to explore "extra-family" interests. However, her eldest-child parents had never been given the "luxury" of self-discovery by their parents, and were not about to condone it for their daughter.

Throughout her childhood and young adulthood, Mary attempted to fulfill her parents desires for her by focusing on activities and behavior that she knew would please them. However, as an adolescent, she became increasingly conflicted and rebellious, and finally made the decision to be "true" to her own natal identity and desires, rather than her parents'.

Mary's chart, (next page), is packed with symbols of an oldest child with her own agenda. Her Twelfth House stellium, (three or more planets in one house), indicates that she is too sensitive and inspired to, in her words, "reduce herself to these meaningless and heartless subjects (business, etc.)". Jupiter retrograde opposing Saturn, (as an oblique retrograde planet), is a classic aspect of firstborns who see themselves as moving in a direction diametrically opposed to that of their parents' beliefs and value systems.

MARY'S CHART

Tropical
Placidus
True Node

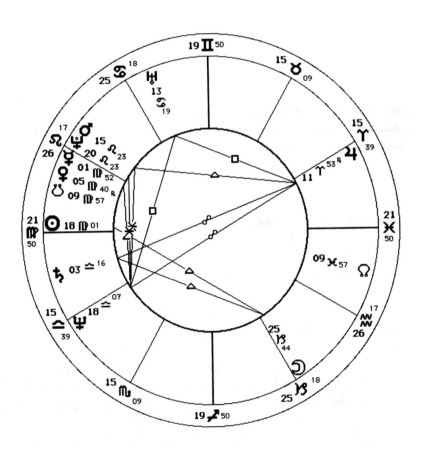

Her Full-Phase opposition suggests Mary's impending rebellion against her father's pressure, in order to assert her own identity which is in direct opposition to her father's. Her Twelfth House Sun and stellium in Virgo suggests that she is looking for an eternal or timeless (Twelfth House) self-expression through her art, which will give purpose (Sun) and inspiration (Twelfth House) to her life.

Her Twelfth House stellium also suggests that she has chosen these particular parents so that she can make a conscious sacrifice (Twelfth House) of the collective opinion, custom and security they represent, in favor of her deeper, more meaningful internal, or spiritual values, which society, and her parents often ridicule as "unreal fantasies".

Mary also discussed that the fact that she had at one time used amphetamines in order to avoid or escape the pain, (Virgo in her chart), caused by her painful, perfectionist, over-achieving (her Capricorn Moon) parental patterning. The Fifth House position of her Moon additionally suggests unfulfilled parental ambitions (Capricorn), and may have contributed to Mary's feeling that she was merely an extension of her parents' unfulfilled creativity and self-expression (Fifth House). And in fact, her Twelfth House Sun in partile semi-sextile to her Neptune suggests that Mary's father had a creative part of himself which was never given free expression.

The transit of the planet Uranus in opposition to itself, in Mary's chart, which is also square to both her Saturn and Jupiter, gives rise to her natal Cardinal T-square between these three planets and the authority issues connected with these aspects. These configurations indicate the adjustment that Mary needed to make in her relationship with her father, viz., how to assert her personal identity, values and desires in the face of his didactic behavioral guidelines and expectations.

Mary's life lesson can be seen here as her need to develop her own self-image (Moon), through her own self-determined efforts (Capricorn), by rebelling (Moon/Uranus opposition) against the authority figure (her father). This self-assertion will lead her to discover her own inner security—another Moon function. The fact that her

Moon is separating from both Uranus and Pluto also suggests that Mary has probably had prior life struggles with this same dynamic of having to claim her own inner values by rebelling against a repressive authority figure(s).

Through astrological counseling, Mary received the "validation" and encouragement she needed to continue on her chosen course of expressing her inner artistic nature, even in the face of her parents' disapproval, which was compounded by her stellium in Virgo (self-doubt). Discussing her firstborn birth order position in relation to her parents' also assisted her in understanding the extremely rigid parental and social expectations and pressures that she had to cope with in her family life.

"Parentification", or taking on a surrogate parent role, is another relationship distortion that commonly occurs to firstborns. Oftentimes, assuming adult roles and responsibilities at an early age leaves the oldest or firstborn child "without a childhood". Some parentification is healthy because it can instill a sense of responsibility and conscience in children. But this positive parentification presupposes that the parents have achieved enough of their own self-identity and independence to eliminate their need for inappropriate emotional or physical support from their children. Asking the children to help out around the house is a positive illustration of parentification—expecting them to take over major parental roles is not.

Requiring a child to act as a surrogate husband or wife, by taking responsibility for a majority of family functions, (cooking, cleaning, childcare, wage-earning, etc.), or expecting a firstborn to vicariously fulfill the parental/family "dreams", are negative, inappropriate forms of parentification.

Many firstborn and eldest children feel that they were somehow forced to grow up too fast, to assume too much responsibility too soon, thus becoming increasingly over-achieving, perfectionistic, and task-oriented as their lives progressed. No matter how socially far they climb, or how much outer success they achieve, these types of firstborn adults seem bereft of inner contentment, joy or peace.

Children who get caught in this web of compliance to unreasonable parental demands usually can not distinguish between what they externally accomplish in their lives and who they really are as individuals. Self-discovery, identity definition and self-expression are crucial issues for firstborns. If they are left unresolved, negative parentification issues may cause major upheavals in oldest-child or firstborn adults' careers, psychological health, relationships, etc.

Firstborn parentified males often become obsessed with accumulating power as adults, especially in response to their father's, "You're not good enough", or "Can't you do better", criticisms, which, unfortunately, may echo down through the corridors of a firstborn male's entire lifetime. Afraid of being perceived as weak or vulnerable, these male firstborns often compensate for their fears by achieving lofty, powerful career positions, from which vantage point they may "hurl" down extremely critical and judgmental opinions—projecting their own damaged internalized father-images onto the people, environment and world around them.

On the other hand, parentified, (parent identified), female firstborns may feel that they have no personal power or life of their own. They may play the role of the eternal victim who lives only to serve the needs of others. Also, parentified firstborn females, like their male counterparts, often feel that they can never successfully fulfill their parent's expectations—they can never take on enough responsibility, do enough or achieve enough to please their parents, family, bosses, friends, etc.

Firstborn daughters, like firstborn sons, frequently become extreme perfectionists, and achieve the highest standards of academic and social performance—honor student, prom queen, class president, corporate president, etc. This is done in an almost frenzied attempt to fulfill their parents' every wish, without, however, any reference whatever to their own emotional and psychological needs and desires. Also, firstborn female adults are often attracted to older male partners as a way of compensating for the love and attention they could never fully win from their fathers.

Attracting "wounded birds"—needy, emotionally or physically deprived people—is another characteristic of the firstborn female who is acting out her unconscious parental dictum: "Don't think of yourself, you're here to help others". This syndrome of wanting to help out every needy person will usually involve the planet Venus in Pisces, the Twelfth House, or in aspect to Neptune; or Neptune will occupy the Seventh House itself.

Astrologically speaking, the signs Cancer or Capricorn on the descendant are likely indicators that firstborn individuals will have a tendency to be attracted to weak, easily controlled mates, on whom they can project their parentally instilled fears of weakness and vulnerability (Cancer). On the other hand, Capricorn on the descendant may indicate that a person selects dominant, authoritative partners in order to externalize their parentally created "weakness" or inadequacy issues: "You'll just never measure up."

For both male and female firstborns, the words "You've done it wrong", may hold an extremely potent, negative emotional charge. Again, this arises from the parents', (particularly, the father's), unrealistic performance expectations and standards. Until this complex is brought into conscious awareness and dealt with, firstborns cannot be freed from the nagging inner sense that they are never quite "perfect", or "good" enough.

Firstborn psychological responses to these inner parent/child conflicts may take the form of a deep sense of inadequacy and failure, "I just couldn't do enough", or a feeling of rejection, or exploitation, "They expected too much from me", or anger, "Dammit, when do I get my turn." Other firstborn mental "parentification scripts" may include, "I'll work myself to death because that's how hard Dad worked", or "I'll never bother to work on myself because others need me too much", or, conversely, "I never got to be a kid". Any or all of these feelings or perceptions may indicate unresolved firstborn birth order role conflicts.

Parentified firstborns often make extremely intolerant parents themselves, because they project their family programming and resentments onto their own children: "Don't be such a baby", or "I never got to act like a kid—why should you." Although firstborns are excellent managers and care-takers, presenting a competent, accomplished face to the world, in reality, their inner emotional lives can be empty and conflicted.

Firstborns can also become lost in their roles as super-responsible, overachieving adults. Many of them will admit that feel alive or "real" only when they are working, producing, managing or taking care of someone. Similar to only children, firstborns usually feel the need to protect and carry on their family traditions, beliefs and rules, and consequently may develop a strong sense of moral responsibility based on their demanding parental expectations.

Because of this intense drive to fulfill parental expectations, firstborns can become "control-heads", needing to impress others, or become over-involved in other people's affairs; or they may try to impose their parents', "We know best", attitude on their own mates, children and society in general.

Studies done on firstborns have revealed that they are usually more conservative in their approach to education and religion, and tend to avoid dangerous or risky activities. Also, firstborns appear to be more depression-prone than their younger siblings. Firstborns form a large majority of completed suicides in the U.S. Another interesting study on a group of 20 Olympic-caliber weight lifters showed that 65% of them were firstborns. This corresponds to the common firstborn perception that it is their responsibility to carry the "weight of the world" on their shoulders.

Because they may be in a state of almost perpetual fear, unconsciously apprehensive of the seen and unseen forces threatening the survival of their family legacy and identity, the firstborn can also be beset by security issues. As a result, they are often "information addicts"—compulsively gathering every known fact about a situation before acting on it or before venturing into unfamiliar territory.

Firstborns are also notorious for "getting the job done"—once they've exhaustively researched all potential liabilities of the situation, that is. Psychologists have speculated that this is the reason why firstborn suicide attempts usually succeed—they're just so good at "getting the job done."

Occasionally, a firstborn, as in Rich's or Mary's case, rebels against parental or social expectations and manifests or acts out the characteristics of Aquarius, i.e., they take a direction in life that is directly contrary to, or the opposite of, their parent's and society's direction or expectations. The life choices that are made under these conditions may not necessarily be appropriate for the rebelling firstborn, however, they can serve the function of removing the person from negative parental and social spheres of influence.

Looking at firstborns from an astrological point of view, it's obvious that they have been severely "overexposed" to Saturn issues (father/authority), the sign Capricorn, (criticism, expectations), and the Tenth House (outer-world accomplishments).

In relation to a firstborn's feelings of being "flawed" or inadequate, look for planets in Virgo or the Sixth House. Firstborn women, for example, with these configurations, may be prone to hatred or resentment of their "weaker" bodies. For instance, if a firstborn woman's menstrual cycles somehow interfere with her ability to get her job done, she may feel a sense of intense guilt, self-hate, frustration and failure, which may then lead to physical illness (Virgo/Sixth House).

It's important for firstborns to be aware of the extreme pressures to perform that may have been exerted on them by their parents. Firstborns need to give themselves permission to be who they really are, to experience vulnerability and need, to learn to love themselves for who they are, rather than for what they do and accomplish in the outer world.

Firstborns many times are literally battered by the often ridiculously unrealistic expectations and demands made on them by their parents, and can benefit tremendously from the same abuse or grief therapies that other types of abused children utilize.

A Moon in Capricorn, the Tenth House, or in aspect to Saturn may indicate that a firstborn is learning to legitimize their true emotions and to express fear and sadness. However, Mercury in Capricorn, the Tenth House or in aspect to Saturn often suggests that a firstborn may be using their highly developed verbal skills to create intellectual "smoke-screens", and to manipulate others, in order to avoid having to expose their inner fear, insecurity and sadness. They may also have internalized their father's projection: "You're not so bright, are 'ya?"

Venus in Capricorn, the Tenth House, or in aspect to Saturn suggests that a firstborn may have become the surrogate spouse for their mother or father, and may have internalized the emotional void that existed between the parents. Other planets in aspect to Saturn in the Tenth House or the sign Capricorn can show that the firstborn may have been "swallowed up" by the father's (Saturn) need to control.

Those firstborns with Saturn and the Moon in dynamic aspect, (conjunction, semi-square, sesqui-quadrate, inconjunct or opposition), may have gotten the subliminal message that they were not wanted by their parents. A child (Moon) who has been rejected (Saturn) from birth, may, as an adult, reject his or her loved ones or children, or be enveloped in chronic depression throughout life as a result of unresolved feelings of parental rejection.

The progressions of the Moon, or transits or progressions to the Moon (the polarity "planet" of Saturn) are focal periods of change in a firstborn's chart. The Moon's contacts to other planets (especially Saturn), may often manifest as crises in the firstborn's life that fulfill his or her worst fears of not being productive, in control or "on-target".

Although perhaps horrifying to the firstborn's rational mind, these Moon transits or "lunar landings" actually offer excellent opportunities for revealing and rectifying distorted attitudes and behavior that they adopted in youth in order to cope with their parental and family expectations and demands. A firstborn's Moon sign also gives clues as to how they experienced their specific home environment, and what emotional responses accompanied their firstborn experience.

Periods involving the Moon's movement and contact to other planets are opportune times for the emotionally repressed firstborn to get in touch with their own natural, internal rhythms, moods and feelings which may have been buried under their negative Saturn (father) influence. Moon cycles are also an excellent time for the firstborn to learn to relax and stop worrying about whether their activities are accomplishing anything.

I also believe that the Saturn/Moon polarity is focal in terms of firstborns learning to blend their unbalanced masculine and feminine sides. Developing a comfortable working relationship with their "dark side of the Moon", or their unconscious mind, assists firstborns in overcoming their exaggerated need to produce (Saturn), and encourages positive self-esteem which is based on their intrinsic worth rather than on their external performance.

The interaction of the Moon and the planet Saturn should be closely watched in the firstborn chart, as they often herald important, critical developmental turning points surrounding the issues of vulnerability, receptivity and openness. In other words, overly responsible, authoritative firstborns, during Moon/Saturn contacts may be confronted with life events that force them into letting down their defenses.

In the simplest sense, the Moon represents the inner child. Firstborns usually have a very deep need to reconnect with their inner child—to listen, understand, and empathize with its feelings, vulnerabilities and needs. In this way, firstborns can begin to feel their lives more intensely, and to experience the innocence, wonder and excitement that the natural child feels.

If a firstborn's horoscope champions an emphasized Tenth House, Saturn, or planets in Capricorn, it may be more difficult for him or her to perceive the relevancy or value in changing their traditional Saturn lifestyle and emotional patterns. If firstborns are externally comfortable with their own super-responsible, caretaking role, as may be the case under the aspects just mentioned, they may find it difficult to initiate individuation or separation therapy. However, with environmental or relationship support, (Moon), firstborns can transfer their feelings of responsibility for others to responsibility for their own lives and well-being, and begin to relinquish the need to look out for everyone else at the expense of their own inner contentment, happiness and personal fulfillment.

Additional difficulties for firstborns are dynamic aspects to

Mars and Saturn. These two planets can represent deep conflicts between what the person **should** do (Saturn-Capricorn), and what he or she **wants** to do (Mars/Aries). This internal conflict may force firstborns into confrontation with often extremely formidable external obstacles and overt rejection when they assert their own identity needs, beliefs or desires within a disapproving family or social environment. And because most firstborns have internalized an illusory, idealized father image (Saturn), their moves toward independent (Mars) self-expression may meet with internal, as well as external opposition.

Reconciling Mars and Saturn can be a painful, frustrating task for firstborns, but in the most positive light, Mars and Saturn in dynamic aspect to each other can inspire a person to be, what Maslow calls "**metamotivated**". In other words, positive reconciliation of the Mars/Saturn conflict can result in firstborns becoming truly authentic, self-defined, autonomous individuals, who fully and dynamically contribute to the evolution of the society in which they function (Saturn).

What is probably one of the most difficult therapy issues for firstborns is the need for them to take responsibility for **themselves**, and for their **entire** reality. It is extremely important for firstborns to deeply examine who they are apart from their parental and social programming and how they can specifically express their own self-identity while still fulfilling their need for authoritative social roles. They also need to sort out and release their parentally imposed attitudes that contribute to their emotional "imprisonment".

Many firstborns find that the extra "weight" of therapeutic confrontation, on top of their already overdeveloped "Atlas syndrome" (carrying the world on their shoulders), is too much to bear. However, once they deal with the all-important issue of letting-go, the therapy process gets easier, and eventually, their playful internal child, which has been buried alive under a mountain of parental demands and responsibilities, can reappear and grace their lives with the happiness and carefree attitude of youth, which so many firstborns so desperately desire to experience.

Counseling Tips for Firstborns: Firstborns need to realize that they may be ultra-sensitive to the criticisms and judgements of others because of the overemphasized and unrealistic expectations and demands made on them by their parents, and in particular, their fathers (Saturn).

Continually reinforce the concept that they do not have to **do**, or accomplish something, in order to be valued and loved for who they are. Emphasize the positive role that the Mars/Saturn dynamic can play in balancing their father/self-identity conflict.

Assist them in viewing and participating in their lunar cycles and rhythms (full Moon meditations, ritual dancing, etc.) as a way of getting in touch with their inner, spiritual nature, as well as their repressed inner child.

Introduce the concept that loving and being loyal to parents does not have to mean following in their fathers' footsteps at the expense of their own identity and needs.

CHAPTER TEN

THE SECOND AND YOUNGEST CHILD

On the subject of second and lastborn children, we are going to limit our overview to secondborns from two and three-child families only. In a **two-child** family, the second child is, obviously, the lastborn or youngest child also, while in the **three-child** family, the secondborn is also a middlechild.

As families grow in size, parents, often through necessity, assign, consciously or unconsciously, specific roles and role tasks to each of their children. As we discussed in the last chapter, firstborns are usually made responsible for sustaining and maintaining their parents' performance expectations. Firstborns are usually aware of the **external** parental demands made on them.

In contrast to externally oriented firstborns, second or lastborn children feel and respond to **inner** pressures and tensions which arise from their acute intuitive sense of underlying family conflicts and stress. The unconscious role assignment of the secondborn is to bring undefined family conflicts to the surface through their actions and behavior. Secondborns play the role of the family "dramatists". For instance, if parents are experiencing unexpressed difficulties in their relationship, their second child will often "act out" the hidden parental conflicts through "bad" or confrontational behavior.

This acting-out usually occurs in response to the secondborn's internal need to reveal and express, for the family as a whole, hidden family issues and underlying tensions that may be causing very real problems on the surface, such as parental arguments and fighting, etc. Should the parents refuse to face the real issues that are causing their second or lastborn child to misbehave, the child may become even more difficult to relate to or control, and may withdraw into a gloomy, bad-tempered emotional shell.

As the rebel or "crazy" child of the family, the second or lastborn is often "dumped on" by parents and siblings and may begin to internalize the family's problems as their own: "Well, it must be me that's the problem—maybe I'm the one that's crazy." As the second or lastborn attempts to cope with these internal conflicts, they may polarize **away** or distance themselves from their real emotions and feelings, and exhibit extremely sober, serious, rational external behavior, becoming aloof and detached from the family circle. In the case of the three-child family, in particular, this scenario is usually responsible for the way in which second or middle-children are emotionally abandoned by their dysfunctional families.

Also, contrary to firstborns, second or lastborns are more influenced by their mothers, as opposed to the dominant father influence in the firstborn scenario. The emotional tone, the criticisms and opinions of the mother primarily effect the attitudes and behavior of secondborns.

The Air/Water polarities of Gemini/Pisces, Cancer/Libra and Scorpio/Aquarius are many times difficult dynamics to negotiate for second and lastborns with these elements in their horoscope. Within a dysfunctional family environment, second and lastborns who have planets occupying any of these three Air/Water dyads may face particularly difficult developmental and emotional issues.

The disturbing emotional undercurrents (Water) in the family that second or lastborns acutely feel may not be consciously identified or labeled (Air). In other words, secondborns often do not realize that their internal conflicts are reflections of their **family's** unresolved issues, rather than their own. They may also be unaware that they have unconsciously polarized away from their own emotions (Water), and adopted a overly rational, detached attitude and orientation (Air) in order to cope with their internal pain arising from their dysfunctional family circumstances.

Planets in the Air element, or in the Third, Seventh or Eleventh Houses are resources that second and lastborns can use, because their influence can assist the secondborn in labeling and identifying (Air) internalized family conflicts and put them in correct perspective. Many times, secondborns who have repressed their emotions will unconsciously assume the burden of carrying a major portion of the family's problems, and in particular, the mother's unexpressed psychological pain, anger and confusion.

Having deeply emotionally bonded with the family's or mother's complexes, most second or lastborns from conflicted family backgrounds find it difficult to admit that they are struggling with their family's issues and not their own, so it is vital that they go through a sorting-out process in order to separate their own psychological and emotional elements from those of their parents and siblings.

The absence of planets in the Air element or in the Third, Seventh or Eleventh Houses in the second or lastborn's chart may, unfortunately, exacerbate the emotional difficulties that they may encounter in a dysfunctional family environment. Without an Air influence, secondborns can feel "drowned" or "pulled under" by the emotional (Water) undercurrents in the family; they may feel "strangled" and unable to articulate or communicate (Air) the pain, fear, tension or anxiety that they feel or sense (Water).

Like a drowning person, gulping water, gasping for air and unable to scream for help, the secondborn without Air elements may become fragmented and disoriented, and a seemingly unbridgeable chasm may develop between their conscious, intellectual and physical functioning and their inner emotional reality.

Secondborn males, especially, are prone to emotional repression, often unconsciously carrying around their internalized damaged mother, or family image far longer than their female counterparts, who, in some ways, are given more permission by society to express, act out and release their painful and conflicted emotions and feelings.

The intense emotional repression which many second or lastborns experience, being a water element issue, will seek an outlet in any way it can. In many cases, the unexpressed emotional blockage manifests in physical abnormalities and illness. Double pneumonia ("drowning"), emphysema, asthma or bed-wetting are examples of how secondborns may physically express and attempt to release unresolved and unacknowledged emotional pain and disturbance.

These "fluidic", Water, or psychosomatic illnesses sometimes will not respond even to drugs or hypnosis, because the "current" of these subterranean rivers of repressed emotional energy have become to strong to be "dammed up" any longer.   Body therapies such as Reichian or Gestalt therapy, or bioenergetics are extremely important and beneficial to secondborns who have an absence of planets in the Air element or the third, Seventh or Eleventh Houses, challenged by Water planets or planets in Water Houses, and to second and lastborns in general.

In these therapies, the body is given an opportunity to express, identify and clear the intense emotional trauma and pain that the intellect can not face or express.   Body-oriented therapies can get secondborns' heads and hearts back on "speaking terms".   Also, it is important for secondborns to develop what Buddhists refer to as the "witness" attitude, which means dispassionately watching and observing emotional turbulence or "winds", without personally identifying with or being swept away by them.

Another important issue involving the secondborn birth position is the desire of two or three-child parents to "homogenize" the family experience so that family life is easier to control.   In other words, individual acting-out and experimentation by the children in a two or three-child family may often be discouraged by the parents because the process of individual identity formation entails more parental attention, time and patience.

Not all parents are willing to have their homes and lives "upset" by their children's free, and almost always, disruptive, expression of their individuality.   When the second child comes along, many parents "stiffen" internally, anticipating the extra work load that an additional child entails.   The parents may feel that they have to "batten down the hatches" for the developmental storm ahead, and they may devise any number of methods for maintaining control over the difficult child rearing issues facing them.

Unfortunately for secondborns, they can be the natural heirs of their parents control fears. Family rules may become stricter, in larger family groups and, especially in tilted (same gender) two or three-child families, the children may be viewed as one homogenous unit by their parents: "You and your sister(s) are just alike—and isn't it wonderful how you both (all) like the same things." Even though this statement may be patently untrue, it reflects the parents' desires to simplify family life by ignoring the multiple, individual needs of the children.

Because of this "homogenization" process, achieving independent status or recognition within the family group can be difficult for secondborns. The lack of self-identity and self-esteem that may result, when combined with the secondborn's sensitivity to emotional undercurrents in the family, can create an extremely challenging developmental situation.

If secondborns have a poorly developed sense of self, they will probably not trust their own perceptions of hidden family problems, and, as a result, instead of asserting that something really is wrong in the family, they may simply accept their parents' "crazy-making" denials such as, "Oh, honey, it's all in your head", or, "You're just imagining things, dear".

Unfortunately, most dysfunctional families have no idea that their secondborns' bad behavior is signalling disturbing and unresolved subliminal family problems, and the secondborn must simply bear the psychological and emotional suffering that the family's denial creates. This circumstance invariably leads to a mind/body split—in other words, the secondborn's body, or intuitive senses indicate that there is family conflict that needs resolution. However, the mind or intellect is being forced to deny the existence of the problem, and has no choice but to "split off" from the body.

This mind/body split is debilitating and destructive and needs to be dealt with through some type of body-oriented psychology which will release the intense frustration and repression created by the collective and self-denial of unresolved family conflicts.

One advantage of being the second of three siblings is that the child has the opportunity to supervise and direct their younger sibling, which gives them a much needed sense of control or dominance. However, if the family is tilted, and all three children are all girls, for instance, the secondborn may experience a sense of having been displaced. After all, with the eldest and baby sisters in the "starring" family roles, who needs the "superfluous" middle daughter? An adult issue for secondborns with this family history is often, "Why don't I belong; I never feel like I really belong anywhere, or have a place in life."

What these types of secondborns usually crave most is a feeling of specialness. They need to be able to feel and believe that they can achieve something unique and distinct for themselves, that they have special ideas and talents that can benefit society or humanity. Parents with two or three children, particularly in tilted families, need to encourage their secondborns to develop their own place in the family and in their social life.

Planets in the Eleventh House, the sign of Aquarius, or an angular Uranus are potentially helpful astrological elements for this birth position. They suggest that the secondborn child will naturally orient him or herself towards unique forms of self-expression which will, in turn, lead them to their own special niche in life. Also, secondborns, unlike firstborns, often have more implicit permission from their parents to explore (Aquarius/Uranus), alternative lifestyles and attitudes—to "blaze new trails".

However, if the child's self-expression is undermined or blocked by the parents, the secondborn may learn to fear or discredit his or her own intuitive perceptions and hunches, and may feel out of place or disoriented in child and adulthood.

From a metaphysical point of view, the lesson for secondborns may be to develop their distinct and separate identities and to verbally express and assert their intuitive perceptions in spite of their parents' denials or "collectivizing" and homogenizing tendencies.

Secondborns are often more concerned with the future, as opposed to firstborns who are more oriented toward the traditional past. Secondborns are also more likely to experiment with alternative lifestyles and new ideas, and may often seek out societal sub-groups or "counter cultures" that give them the sense of place and identity that they missed in their family experience. However, secondborns with Uranus retrograde in their charts, are likely to find their own unique place or self-identity apart from any other peer group, no matter how progressive or radical it might be.

Transits of Uranus to the foreground or to the personal planets, Sun, Mercury, Venus, Mars and especially to the Moon, may herald the beginning of a family "de-conditioning" process for the secondborn. Transits of other planets to natal Uranus, the Eleventh House or to planets in Aquarius also suggest an on-going process of "shedding" the family past.

Suppressed images or feelings from youth will often surface during these transits; disassociated images and irrational emotions may also arise, indicating the "softening" of the secondborn's psychological defense mechanisms.

Natally, Eleventh House planets, planets in the sign Aquarius or an angular Uranus suggest the secondborn's need to liberate him or herself from the family's homogenizing influence and denials which make secondborns appear radical or crazy to themselves and others.

Let's examine some specific examples of secondborn birth order dynamics, beginning with the situation of a younger Pisces brother of an aggressive Aries eldest brother—(B)B—in a two-child family. This secondborn male child will probably face intense issues of dominance and competition with his eldest firstborn brother, especially if the age gap between them is three years or less. Because the eldest brother has been a pampered only child for several years he has a well-developed sense of self-identity and an extremely well-defined place in the family. With the birth of the second child, the sibling birth order positioning might be advantageous to the firstborn Aries brother, who enjoys the sensation of having a younger brother to dominate and control.

The secondborn brother, who is naturally at an age disadvantage in the relationship, may feel that he is completely overshadowed by his older, more experienced, autonomous brother and may simply "give up the fight" for his own personal power and identity. If the sibling relationship has not been moderated by the parents, this secondborn male could become extremely anti-social, rebellious or even self-destructive as a result of his repeated failures to "best" his brother, and to define and claim his own identity and place in the family.

The image that this secondborn brother of two brings to my mind is the "misunderstood, oversensitive, wounded-underdog young male misfit," Hollywood hero immortalized by James Dean.

If the planet Mars (the ruler of brothers) aspects this secondborn's south node, his self-destructive anger might become even more exaggerated. Unconsciously, he may attract underdogs or "wounded birds" who reflect his own victimized self-image.

Planets in the Sixth or Twelfth House, or in the signs Virgo or Pisces might suggest that a secondborn brother has bonded with a worrying, fearful or pessimistic mother, and his Mars/Pluto or Mars/Saturn aspects may indicate that he is fighting his mother's battles in his own relationships. Additionally, his Capricorn or Tenth House Moon may suggest that he is fearful of expressing his emotions and vulnerabilities, even though they may not be entirely his own.

Intense sibling rivalry between older and secondborn brothers may, if unchecked, lead to open warfare. This dynamic is vividly illustrated by the life of the real estate tycoon, Donald Trump, himself a secondborn son, whose firstborn eldest brother "failed" to fulfill his father's career expectations. Trump's father, in fact, encouraged open, explicit, almost vicious competition between Donald and his older brother for inheritance of the Trump family fortune and name—apparently, Donald "won". The entire world has been witness to the type of insensitive aggression that can develop when "Cain and Abel" are pitted against each other by their parent(s) in a battle for dominance and control.

As another example of secondborn dynamics, we'll take the case of a younger sister of a brother—(B)S—which reflects a more "ideal" and traditional family structure. If the parents in this family are comfortable with traditionally defined dominant husband and sub-ordinate wife roles, this secondborn sister will probably be comfort-able in her birth order role also.

However, if the mother is dissatisfied with her passive feminine role and feels that she has somehow missed out in her marriage, she may be become jealous of her daughter's position as the "darling girl" of the family, and resent her successes and enjoyment of life. As the younger sister of a brother, this secondborn daughter may feel comfortable with masculine values, and non-traditional female lifestyles, especially if she has planets in Aries, Sagittarius or Aquarius. In this case, she may be more outgoing, athletic and popular than her mother was in her youth, all of which might fuel her mother's emotions of jealousy and resentment, isolation, betrayal and insecurity.

In this situation, the mother may attempt to continually undermine her daughter's self-confidence and free, adventurous, easy-going attitude. She might place restrictive rules and demands on her daughter in order to prevent her from expressing her extraverted, nature, or she may try to lay "guilt trips" on the girl, making her feel that she is being "disloyal" to her mother by expressing her own identity.

In these circumstances, the secondborn daughter needs to psychologically reinforce her right to assert her own identity and reality and to avoid identifying with her mother's "sour grapes" attitude by enjoying and expressing her own special birth order advantages.

The younger brother of a sister—(S)B— can be one of the most challenging birth order relationships, specifically because this structure does not conform to the traditional male role of dominance, control, etc. Younger brothers of older sisters may feel insecure and undefined about their masculinity, and may compensate by overemphasizing their masculine traits in their relationships later in life.

A younger sister of a brother may look for an older brother of a younger sister for a mate, or a passive female model that allows him to dominate and control the relationship. His Moon or Venus in signs such as Taurus, Cancer or Pisces may suggest that he is more likely to project his unbalanced masculinity into his personal relationships. The Moon or Venus in dynamic aspect to his Sun or Mars also suggests that this younger brother may find it difficult to integrate his feminine side.

The relationship of this secondborn brother of an older sister to his father is extremely important. If the father is a well-balanced masculine role model, his presence will help the child mitigate the perhaps "smothering" feminine influence of the older sister and mother. However, if the father is too macho or too effeminate, his son's gender identity will most likely be confused as well. Secondborn males in this birth order position would benefit from work in men's "Robert Bly" style therapy groups, where they can learn to better define and integrate balanced internal male/female roles and relationships.

In the case of a younger sister of an elder daughter—(S)S—in a family of two, the younger may often be more intellectually or cognitively developed than the older. However, the secondborn can see her older sister as a paragon or ideal role model, even though her sisterly devotion may not be reciprocated by her eldest sister. Hard aspects by other planets to Venus (ruler of sisters) may reflect a slave/master or teacher/student relationship between the first and secondborn sisters. The secondborn female is likely to duplicate this relationship in her interactions with female authority figures later in life.

The secondborn sister may also feel very distant from her father, in that there are already two other females in the family (her mother and elder sister) "jockeying" for his love and attention. The younger sister can feel "left in the dust" when it comes to being part of the intimate triangle relationship formed by her father, mother and eldest sister. A secondborn daughter with this background may attract this same triangulated type of relationship conflict in her adult life, in which she is forever competing with two other females in order to get the masculine attention and love she needs.

Additionally, because of the two-child, tilted nature of her family (all female children), this secondborn daughter may also be in intense competition with her older sister in establishing her own separate identity within her tilted (same-gender) family.

Also, the elder sister in this situation may feel jealous and resentful of her younger sister, perceiving her as the pampered baby of the family who seems to always "get away with more." Firstborns frequently feel that more is expected of them than their younger siblings—that all the family responsibilities are on their shoulders, and that they never get to simply play or indulge in the carefree fun that the younger children are allowed to have.

As a result, the younger sister may have to deal with possible undermining behavior from her elder sister—"You can't ever do anything right", or "You're always such a baby about everything".

The secondborn daughter of a tilted two-child family, like her male, younger brother of a brother counterpart, needs to find an environment which encourages her self-expression and self-definition, especially if the family discouraged her separate identity development. She also needs to be aware of her possible worshipful attitude towards older, authoritative females who duplicate her elder sister's possible "slave master" role.

Moving on to the three-child family, the secondborn in this family structure is also the middlechild, which means that he or she may also have exaggerated identity issues. Being sandwiched between the firstborn and the baby of the family, the secondborn or middleborn is likely to feel left out, and robbed of a well-defined, meaningful place and identity within the family group. If the three-child family is also tilted (same gender children), the secondborn is even more at risk in terms of opportunities for fulfilling identity development.

All in all, secondborns in dysfunctional two or three-child families can experience the most emphasized self-identity issues of any of the other birth order positions, especially if the child is a second-gender son or daughter, in which case, they may be devalued as "just another daughter (or son)".

Another identity issue that can develop for a secondborn daughter centers around her relationship with her mother. Because the firstborn sister or brother is usually dominantly bonded with the father, the secondborn tends to gravitate towards the mother, often closely bonding with her mother's emotional and psychological issues, at the expense of her own identity needs and development.

A secondborn female client who came to me for counseling had experienced this mother/daughter dynamic in her childhood. She told me that, in her adult life, she was feeling extremely frustrated because she never seemed to get the emotional support she needed from her relationships. In looking at her chart, we discovered that she had Cancer rising and her Moon (its ruler) was positioned in Cancer in her Eleventh House.

I suggested to her that these elements indicated that her own mother may have felt guilty about her lack of maternal love for her secondborn daughter. My client admitted that she had always felt that her mother was not "there" for her, and that she, the daughter, was somehow responsible for emotionally supporting her mother, rather than her mother supporting her.

Secondborns, because of their closeness to their mothers, will often have an idealized mental image of her—the mother who can "do no wrong". When the mother somehow fails in her role as a paragon, the secondborn may attempt to sustain her image by taking on the burden of the mother's emotional or psychological issues in order to support her and hopefully disguise the mother's weaknesses.

Adult secondborn daughters involved in this dynamic will understandably have difficulty in attracting relationships that support their own needs, and for this reason, it is important for them to psychologically separate their real mother from their idealized mother image. Once this separation process begins, it becomes easier for secondborns to define their own needs, and to make relationship and life choices that are fulfilling and supportive.

Mars in a secondborn daughter's horoscope may suggest that the she has taken on the mother's sexual issues at the expense of her own gender identity. The planet Saturn in dynamic aspect to the Moon's nodes may indicate that the secondborn is carrying guilt about having "spoiled" or interrupted her mother's career plans (the second child often does make it harder for the mother to work). This aspect can result in career "jumping" on the part of the secondborn daughter who feels that she does not deserve to succeed in a career because she ruined her mother's career opportunities.

"Susan", a secondborn daughter with three closely age-spaced brothers, came to me for astrological counseling. Her life issues, typical for secondborns, centered around her parents' and siblings relationships. In reviewing her chart, (next page), after discussing her family history, I noted her Tenth House south node in Taurus. This

SUSAN'S CHART

Tropical
Placidus
True Node

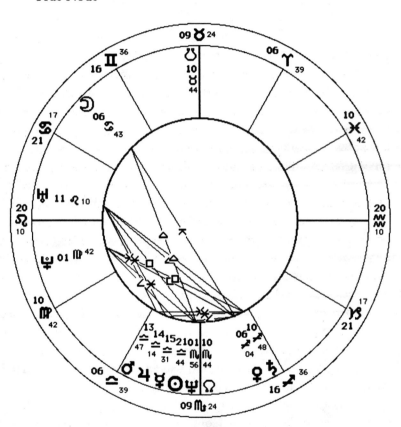

indicated to me, that, in common with most secondborns, Susan had assumed the role of maintaining the stability and cohesiveness of her family's inter-relationships.

At the time of our first counseling session, Susan was 32 years old, unmarried, and living with her parents. She had also experimented with several different careers, none of which seemed "to fit". Her family history revealed that she was the only and oldest female child, with three younger brothers. Her father was an only child, while her mother was the youngest in a family of three children, which, traditionally, is quite compatible, because the only child (the father in this case) is generally comfortable in being the leader, while the youngest (Susan's mother) is accustomed to being led.

Susan remarked that she knew and strictly obeyed her parents' explicit family rules: "Do things the way we tell you to do them", "Never talk about your feelings", and "Take part in primarily 'masculine' activities". Looking at her south node, ruled by Venus in the Fourth House conjoined Saturn, which are each square Pluto, we get an idea of Susan's possible prior-life dependency issues (Fourth House Saturn) and her developmental challenges revolving around the building of her own identity and reality.

Her Cancer Moon also points to her close connection to her dependent mother, and she, admittedly, has always had a difficult time in separating or distancing herself from her mother.

Susan's family was also centrifugal, or extraverted in orientation—wealthy and image-concious. Susan's Libra planets predisposed her to adapting to her parents values without necessarily examining their significance in the light of her own identity needs. This is indicated by her First House Pluto, which suggests that her present life mission is to discover her own identity independent of her family's beliefs, values, traditions, etc.

Her Sun, sextile the ascendant also points to the fact that it was easy (sextile) for Susan to adopt the role of maintaining the family's social image, even despite difficult internal family issues (her mother's alcoholism). Knowing what to say and when to say it (Third House) came naturally (sextile) to her, and was one of her secondchild functions in maintaining the family's stability.

The south node of the Moon in dynamic aspect (inconjunct) to her natal Venus and Saturn (both in the sign Sagittarius), underscores Susan's difficulty in separating her identity and functioning from her mother's. This configuration also indicates that Susan's own mother had not successfully separated from her mother (Susan's Tenth House south node, ruled by her Fourth House Venus in Sagittarius), and had reattached to family life too soon by marrying for security reasons (Fourth House Venus and Saturn).

Susan's life mirrors her mother's issues extremely closely, and conforms to her secondborn female birth role of shouldering her parent's unresolved psychology. It may well be for this reason that Susan has never married, because she has always felt that it is her duty and responsibility to enable her alcoholic mother by giving her attention and loyalty to her rather than to a husband or a successful career.

It is common for a secondborn to be so wed to their parents' value system (Venus, Seventh House), that they are continually led back home, and figuratively, or, as in Susan's case, literally, drawn back into a regressive home environment. In Susan's chart, the Fourth House Venus inconjunct the nodes and co-ruler of the Seventh House, Saturn, (also in her Fourth House) reflect this "returning to the fold" process.

Secondborns need to find their own place in life, to extricate themselves from their parents' or siblings' issues and problems, and to define what they individually value and believe in, as opposed to their family's beliefs and values. Planets in the sign Libra and those in the Seventh House are "notorious" for accentuating a person's inclination to adopt and integrate primarily external values.

In Susan's case, I suggested that she begin to talk with her parents about her feelings that she was not living her own life, and to examine her co-dependent relationship with her mother in the light of her combined family history and personal astrology. Several months after our first consultation, Susan reported to me that she was receiving more emotional support from her family, and was building more of a life of her own.

At the time of our second consultation in April, (about four months after the first), Susan's Jupiter transit was just about to conjoin her Moon (in relation to its Eleventh House position), and transit Uranus was returning for a final opposition in September of that same year. I suggested to her that these transits represented powerful opportunities to increase her awareness (opposition) of her dependency on her mother's value and belief systems. The Uranus opposition to her Moon also represented a supreme opportunity to separate her own emotions and needs from those of her mother and family.

Another case study that strongly illustrates the secondborn's strong maternal bonding, is that of "Roger", a middle-aged salesman who came to me for astrological career counseling. Roger had experienced a long succession of unsatisfying and unsuccessful career choices and several bouts of mild anxiety and depression as a result of his feeling that his life was "going nowhere".

What was immediately evident to me after first reviewing his chart, (next page), was the current transit of Pluto to his Fifth House Saturn in Scorpio and a Saturn transit to his Seventh House Moon in Capricorn, suggesting that Roger's immediate needs were to find and commit to a structure (Capricorn) or environment that reflected his own identity and growth process. His Moon in a Yod with his Venus and Pluto, indicated that Roger had previously (in a past life), experienced a deep psychological and emotional crisis, because he had failed to make the effort commit to a challenging or growth-promoting career that would have enhanced his self-definition.

In looking at his family history, Roger's Twelfth House Venus and Mercury in Gemini conjoined his south node inconjunct his Moon, indicating that he had been unable to articulate or communicate (Gemini) his unconscious conflicts regarding his mother's dissatisfaction about her role as mother and wife.

In effect, Roger, as a child, had "picked up" his mother's disappointment about the "limitations" which Roger, her second child, placed on her life. Her career expectations had been somewhat

ROGER'S CHART

Tropical
Placidus
True Node

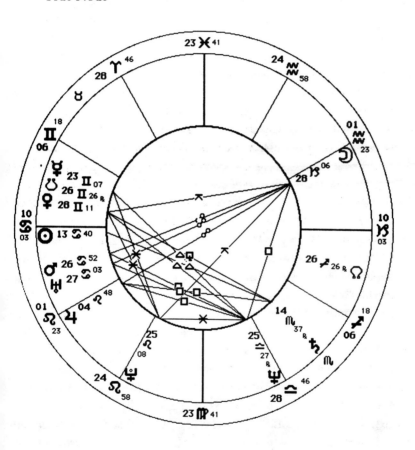

inhibited by her early marriage and first child, however, with the birth of her second son, Roger, she had been "forced" to give up all of her career aspirations. Naturally, Roger was unconsciously deeply affected by his mother's disappointment, and he compensated for his undefined guilt by living out portions of her psychology.

For instance, his Capricorn Moon opposing his First House Mars/Uranus conjunction in Cancer indicates that Roger vicariously plays out his mother's unexpressed rebel role, by rebelling against imposed and unwanted responsibilities. This childhood role has been translated in Roger's adult life as his inability to commit to any career responsibility for any length of time. Also, the fact that Roger duplicated his mother's secondborn birth status (she was the second of two sisters), intensified his maternal bonding and further contributed to his need to act out her personal issues.

A different compensation scenario for this same issue might be a secondborn assuming the consummate career-achievement role in order to fulfill his mother's unmet career aspirations. However, Roger's First House stellium in Cancer disposes him to a fear-of-commitment compensatory behavior, as opposed to the super-achiever attitude that might have developed under different astrological aspects.

Another difficult issue in this scheme is Roger's Cancer/Capricorn axis which points to his natal opposition to his mother's character. The Air and Water elements in his chart also oppose or rival each other, illustrating Roger's mind/emotion or mind/body split that occurred over his conflict between what he felt he should do, (carry the burden of his mother's career disappointments), as opposed to what he really wanted to be in his life. He was in fact, an extraverted personality, whereas his mother was introverted; he was something of a spendthrift, whereas his mother was thrifty, etc.

So, in reality, although he was intimately bonded to her psychological problems, Roger also polarized, or opposed her identity characteristics. Essentially, Roger's maternal relationship resulted in a split in his own psychology—trying to act out his mother's problems and identity, while at the same time, internally opposing her values and beliefs.

I referred Roger to Reichian or bioenergetic body integration work in order to deal with his Air/Water or mind/body split. Additionally, his south node conjoined Mercury in the Twelfth House pointed to an urgent need for dreamwork, in order to contact his very active unconscious life. And because he was still so obviously bonded to his prior-life career and commitment issues, I recommended that he try past-life therapy work also.

Counseling Tips for Second and Youngest: Because of the mind/body (Air/Water) split that may apply here, observing the "body language" of the person when exploring family history issues may reveal feelings that the secondborn is unable to verbally express. Offer body-oriented therapies as an alternative to strictly mental or verbal self-exploration techniques.

Introduce the possibility that their inner conflicts may not necessarily be their own, and explore their mother's unresolved issues and conflicts that they might be mirroring. Allow the second or youngest to ask questions, rather than offering a barrage of unsolicited information.

CHAPTER ELEVEN

THE THIRD AND MIDDLE CHILD

While the firstborn is involved in carrying out the explicit commands of the father, and the secondborn is busy dramatizing subliminal family conflicts, the third child, meanwhile, is usually occupied in defining and mediating inter-relationships within the family group.

The third child, who is also the youngest in a three-child family, or in the middle in a large family, is extremely sensitive to particular **connections** between family members, and attempts to harmonize, mediate and maintain these relationships. In other words, thirdborns are the "referees" of the family. The parental relationship, in particular, is of extreme importance to the thirdborn, and much of the child's self-esteem and self-worth is dependent upon the health and harmony of the parents' interactions.

Thirdborns, middleborns, or the youngest of three children need to feel that everything between their parents and siblings is "OK". If there is disharmony or conflict between family members, especially the parents, the third or youngest child is usually the most affected, and they may openly exhibit their anxiety and fears about possible strained or failed family relationships in order to draw attention to the problems. Thirdborns are similar to secondborns in that they use disruptive or "bad" behavior as a means of attracting attention to unacknowledged family conflicts.

Third and youngest children often take on the psychological qualities of their parental relationship, or of one particular parent. For instance, if one parent is dominant and abusive to the other, the youngest or third child will usually identify with the abused parent and act out that parent's "victim" role. This underdog role comes "naturally" to youngest children who often already feel overpowered by their older, more experienced family members.

Another example of this parental/thirdborn role transference is the youngest child who becomes the "favorite" of an alcoholic or emotionally disturbed parent. The youngest or thirdborn, as the "baby" of the family, may unconsciously reflect a dysfunctional parent's emotionally arrested or "infantile" psychological state, so there may be a strong attraction or bond between the youngest child and an emotionally immature parent.

Because of this bond, the thirdborn child often tries to mediate the dysfunctional parent's relationships with other family members, taking the parent's "side", protecting and defending the parent from family criticism, hostility or demands.

Because of the complex role mixing in which thirdborns or youngest children might be involved or "lost", they are prone to difficult self-identity issues. Planets in Libra or the Seventh House hold keys to thirdborn and youngest-child identity issues because these planets indicate how the person connected to their parent's or siblings inter-relationships.

For example, if Pluto occupies their Seventh House in Virgo, in a thirdborn's chart, this configuration suggests that the child may have shouldered the major impact of their parents' emotional or sexual imbalances or conflicts. Consequently, the child may have become an extension or symbol to his or her family of the unbalanced quality of the parents' relationship.

Because of this, the conflicted parents may unconsciously project their own feelings of anger, pain or rage onto their symbolic "scapegoat"—their thirdborn or youngest, who then internalizes the parents anger. This dynamic many times will physically manifests as chronic illness in the child, or in sullen, deeply withdrawn behavior.

If the thirdborn or youngest child is female, under this same configuration (Pluto occupying her Seventh House Virgo), she may be unconsciously "chosen" by her father to fill the sexual vacuum (Pluto) or compensate for the lack of intimacy that exists between her parents. She may assume the emotional or sexual role as surrogate wife to her father, and perceive her family role as the mediator who "keeps the peace" between the mother and father so that the family can continue to function.

Many planetary oppositions in a chart may suggest that a person perceived his or her parents as polarized, or opposed, in their opinions, values and beliefs. The thirdborn or youngest, in this instance, may feel that it is his or her task to "pull" the two opposing parental figures back together.

Also, if one parent appears stronger or more dominant than the other, thirdborns or youngest can feel that the parental inequities are somehow their fault, and they may try to compensate for them by creating and attracting the same imbalances in their own relationships. It is important for thirdborns and youngest adults and children to continually sort out what parental or family conflicts and issues they may be identifying with and acting out in their own lives. The rulers of the Fourth and Tenth Houses and their positions within the horoscope may also identify other areas or aspects of their psychology which have become polarized, or in other words, are opposing each other.

Female thirdborns with two older brothers are frequently dependent types, who are often easily overpowered or dominated as adults, especially if the brothers are insensitive to their younger sister's own strengths and feminine qualities. Youngest female siblings as adults, often attract or seek out strong, stable, anchoring, masculine mates who duplicate their relationship with their brothers. The issue here is that the thirdborn or youngest female needs to **independently** define and express her identity and femininity, as opposed to having it interpreted for her by her brothers or her adult male partners.

Dependency issues can also arise for thirdborns or youngest children in general. If they do not receive the loving, nurturing concern and reassurance they need from parents and siblings, they may seek dependent roles in their adult relationships which seem to provide the security and attention they missed in their childhood.

In contrast to firstborns, who often have an overemphasized Saturn and underemphasized Moon, thirdborn or youngest children frequently have just the opposite stressed in their psychologies. Whereas firstborns may be too "tough", (Saturn), their youngest siblings are often too "thin-skinned" , overprotected and vulnerable, (Moon). The Moon, in the case of youngest children, may exaggerate their innate sensitivities. For instance, a thirdborn or youngest with a Taurus Moon may be financially irresponsible and dependent on others, rather than strong-willed and self-supporting as the sign Taurus often indicates.

Similarly, A Gemini Moon thirdborn or youngest sibling may become an "eternal child", unable to focus on or commit to anything for any length of time. A Pisces Moon youngest child might become "spaced out" or feel directionless, in response to their inner victim, or defeatist psychology inherited from a parent: "What's the use of trying, I'm not going to get anywhere anyway?"

Because of the family mediator role to which thirdborns and youngest are prone, the Libra side of Venus, or planets in the sign Libra or the Seventh House are important elements in their horoscopes. Pluto, Scorpio and the Eighth House also directly tie into their psychology in that they feel most threatened by confining situations which seem to limit their choices or options (Pluto, Scorpio, Eighth House).

Youngest or thirdborns from dysfunctional homes often have a fear of being trapped in circumstances beyond their control—they had no choice or influence over resolving the conflicts between their parents, and situations which mirror this same dynamic create anxiety and fear for them.

Periods during which planets transit the Eighth House may also bring feelings of powerlessness and insecurity to the surface, reflecting, again, the youngest child's perception that he or she was powerless to change or mediate their parents' conflicts.

Planets in the sign Leo or the Fifth House may suggest that the thirdborn or youngest will do whatever is needed, even dramatic or dangerous acting-out, in order to direct the family's attention to internal relationship problems.

Adult thirdborn or youngest children who feel victimized, dependent and insecure, need to closely examine their family history and family inter-relationships as possible sources of their insecurities and dependency issues, rather than continuing to see themselves as hapless victims who, for no apparent reason, "never get the love and security they need."

Male thirdborns with two older sisters may try to compensate for their feelings of being overpowered or "smothered" by their older female siblings by developing "macho" or "superman" type personalities. A youngest brother with a Pisces or Cancer Moon in dynamic aspect to the Sun and/or Mars may feel fearful or ashamed of his vulnerabilities or weaknesses, and might compensate by emphasizing his overkill approach to his masculinity. Therapies that deal with balancing masculine and feminine energies are beneficial in these instances.

In certain family structures, the thirdborn or youngest role may be assumed by another sibling. For instance, a secondborn female child may take the thirdborn role of the go-between, or referee of the family, if her youngest sibling is a brother, because this thirdborn brother may refuse to take the more passive role of family mediator, so his secondborn sister assumes the role in his place. Or, if the family is tilted (same gender children), the youngest and eldest children may bond, leaving the middlechild to assume the mediator or scapegoat role that is usually played by the thirdborn.

In the Tweety Bird/Sylvester cat cartoon version of this birth order dynamic, Tweety Bird (the youngest, thirdborn "family member") and Bulldog (the oldest) have worked out a nice, comfortable "sibling" relationship that is marred only by the presence of the interfering Sylvester, (the secondborn middlechild), who relentlessly creates havoc by trying to "swallow-up" (middlechild jealousy) the youngest "child", vulnerable little Tweety Bird. In this situation, Sylvester assumes the youngest-child role as the family scapegoat and usually gets beaten to a pulp by his bonded eldest and youngest "siblings", who, at the end, go serenely on their way.

Another developmental challenge for thirdborns may arise when the child assumes the guilt for his or her parents difficult or failed relationship. The thirdborn in this situation may react as only children often do to a strained parental relationship: "If only I were a better child, my parents would love each other more, and wouldn't have broken up." At times, youngest and thirdborn children in their role as family mediator, are used as referees by their parents in their disputes, causing severe emotional trauma. Youngest or thirdborn children who have been traumatized in this way may find it extremely difficult to form intimate, trusting, loving relationships throughout their lives.

Thirdborn or youngest children whose horoscopes contain a preponderance of oppositions or foreground oppositions may have been exposed to these types of parental pulls. Being caught between two opposing forces, (or polarized planets), the thirdborn or youngest too often feels responsible for the success or failure of his or her mediating efforts. Thirdborns from dysfunctional family backgrounds may have a sense of being torn apart by family conflicts and often feel that they can never find any middle ground or balance point on any issues at any time in their lives.

If a chart shows the Sun occupying or ruling the Seventh House, or in aspect to Venus, it can indicate that the thirdborn or youngest may be caught or psychologically stuck in trying to reconcile or heal the breach in their parents' relationship. A male thirdborn in this situation often projects this into his marriage or romantic relationships by forcing or demanding that his partner act out compromising or compensatory resolution roles that he, as a child, wanted his parents to play.

A youngest or thirdborn woman, conversely, may act out this dynamic by attracting a "womanizer" male whose infidelity or unfaithfulness in the relationship reflects her own feelings of being abandoned as a result of her parents irreconcilable differences.

Physical loss of one or both of the parents through death or divorce is often much more emotionally devastating to youngest and thirdborn children than to their elder siblings. In addition to the physical loss, the thirdborn or youngest child must also deal with the loss of the family's focal interactive parental relationship, in which so much of their own role identity is invested. So in a sense, this child experiences two major losses—the physical loss and the loss of their family role identity. In some cases, this may be an inconsolable tragedy with which the youngest or thirdborn is unable to cope.

Case in point, a personal friend of mine, who I knew throughout my high-school years, was the youngest thirdborn male in a family of three. His parents **both** died within a few weeks of each other when he was in his late twenties. Only a few years after the death of his parents, my friend also died—apparently by suicide.

Psychodrama, which assists a person in identifying, and relating to polarized elements in the psyche, is an excellent therapeutic method for relieving thirdborns' "referee stress". It can also enable them in giving back to their parents and siblings the responsibility for resolving their own conflicts—a task which rightfully belongs to them, not to the thirdborn or youngest child.

In examining the real life dynamics of a youngest or thirdborn child, we'll look at the case study of "Brad", a male thirdborn in his mid-thirties, who had grown up in a west coast family of three children. He and his two older brothers were closely age-spaced, so their birth order roles were well defined. Brad, as the thirdborn or youngest of the family was tremendously impacted by his parents' relationship, which was very tense and conflicted, although this was never explicitly expressed. In his role as the family "mediator", Brad had been under a great deal of pressure in his attempts to smooth over and "fix" his parents failing relationship.

Brad's father was a music teacher, a professional musician, and an only child of alcoholic parents. His mother was a rather introverted, reserved younger sister of an older brother, and a talented pianist herself. The primary conflict in Brad's parents' relationship arose, not from any birth order incompatibility, but rather from the fact that Brad's mother felt that she had married too young and had not made the right relationship and lifestyle choices.

Of all their three children, only Brad appeared to inherit his parents' musical ability, and his musical interest and talent became the "tool" which he used to try to bring his estranged parents back together.

Brad's strong Water and Earth elements in his chart (next page)

BRAD'S CHART

Tropical
Placidus
True Node

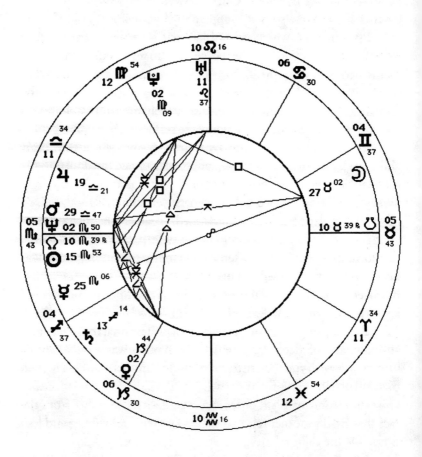

suggest that he would be sensitive to and deeply feel the unspoken conflicts between his parents, but would be reluctant to talk about them to anyone. His emotional repression reflected his entire family's repressive attitude—no one in the family wanted to own up to or confront the tension and pain that the parents were experiencing because of the unresolved conflicts in their relationship.

His Sun/Moon opposition encouraged Brad's thirdborn tendency to bond with his parents and assume the responsibility for their imbalances. Additionally, his Mercury in Scorpio opposing his Moon emphasized his desire to act as the family's "psychologist", and counselor. The Mercury (analytical) element in Brad's chart can be seen as contributing to his development as an extremely critical, mentally oriented adult, divorced from his emotions and feelings.

Brad's Seventh House south node indicates his natural talent for sensing the unspoken dynamics of his parents' relationship. This configuration might also point to prior life (south node) confrontations with this same issue of defining himself through other people's relationships as opposed to dealing with his own identity issues.

The Twelfth House Mars in Libra conjoined Neptune in Brad's chart points to his admitted identity confusion— "I don't know who I really am" , (Mars in the Twelfth House), which stemmed primarily from his feelings of having failed his parents by being another and last male child, rather than the daughter that they would have preferred.

Brad's parents finally divorced when he was 14, leaving him emotionally shaken and traumatized. He felt responsible and blamed himself for his parents' divorce because he perceived that he had failed in his role as family mediator. Brad had ultimately been unable to fix the rift between his parents, even despite his exhaustive efforts, and the family, as a result was left broken and fatherless—a major defeat for a thirdborn.

Several years of self-destructive behavior ensued following Brad's parents' divorce, as he relentlessly continued to punish himself for having failed his parents and family. However, at about age 27, when his natal Tenth House Pluto conjoined his Mars, Brad, (after several years of intensive psychotherapy and various types of bodywork), began to dramatically sever (Mars) his loyalty ties (Mars) to his dysfunctional family past and the pain and guilt associated with it.

At this time, Brad quit his parentally patterned career as a professional musician and began to experiment with other career choices (Tenth House).

Brad's Scorpio rising and north node suggest that his freedom (First House) from his family past in this life symbolizes (Scorpio) his landmark breaking away from his habitual (south node) referee role. In other words, Brad, after probably many lifetimes of identifying himself through other people's relationships, in this life, has found a new (north node) method of self-definition apart from his family programming.

During his Pluto transit opposing his Moon (several months after our first consultation), Brad related to me that he felt he had made significant strides in understanding how he habitually attracted relationships that mirrored his parents' unbalanced and conflicted interactions.

In fact, Brad realized that his father loved and wanted his wife more than she wanted him, (a Pluto abandonment issue), and Brad, in his adult life, had attracted women who reflected his mother's (Moon) loveless attitude towards his father.

It was an important step for Brad, particularly during this Pluto transit, to confront and deal with this issue, because, in a sense, his painful relationships with women who mirrored his mother's conflicts simply provided another way of punishing himself for his parents' failed marriage.

Both transits of and progressions to Pluto, planets in the sign Scorpio and the Eighth House represent excellent opportunities to re-experience parental and sibling interactions and relationship patterns. The "Plutonian" periods in a thirdborn or youngest's life may seem very threatening, painful and emotionally disruptive, but they can likewise be the periods of greatest healing and transformation when experienced within an appropriately supportive or therapeutic environment.

Counseling Tips for Third and Middleborns: These individuals frequently feel powerless (Pluto/Scorpio/Eighth House) to control crucial relationships in their lives, and may end up feeling psychologically defeated and divided (Pluto, Scorpio and Eighth House).

The House location of planets in the sign Scorpio will often point to the specific area or "department" of the thirdborn's, middlechild's, or youngest's life (career, home life, etc.), which they feel most powerless to control or change. These House placements can also suggest the areas in which the person may experience the most transformation and letting go of the past.

For example, planets in Scorpio in the Third or Ninth Houses indicate that an effective release of past trauma, or a personal metamorphosis could be brought about through movement or dance therapy (Feldenkrais technique). Planets in Scorpio in the Fifth House indicate that art therapy or Jungian sand-box therapy would be extremely beneficial in the letting-go or empowering process for thirdborn, middleborn or youngest child issues. Planets in Scorpio in the First House suggest that intense physical work and exercise, or rebirthing and rolfing would be most effective.

Be creative in suggesting a variety of options and solutions to any issues that come up, as thirdborns and middle children feel most powerful when offered a variety of choices, alternatives or solutions to situations.

CHAPTER 12

THE "ONLY" CHILD

The only child is a unique birth order position, being the single position in which the child has complete, one-on-one, unobstructed access to the parents. As the sole object of the parents' time, attention, resources, energy and expectations, the only child has a unique opportunity to benefit from his or her birth order position, depending on the quality of the home environment created by their mother and father.

Another intriguing aspect of only children, that I've found to be true in my practice, is that they can actually mirror **any** of the birth order positions, regardless of the fact that they have no siblings. The focal or prominent planets in an only child's horoscope will usually suggest which birth order position the child has psychologically connected to in response to their family environment. Reviewing these astrological elements may help the only child to discover how he or she is acting out their own or other birth order characteristics in their childhood or adult lives.

Naturally, only children have the tendency to play the role of the oldest child, especially if the parents overtly express their social, academic and career expectations for their sole "heir". The second-born birth order might be assumed if an only child feels that his or her birth was an "accident"—that he has no place in the family because his parents didn't really want him. This attitude reflects the characteristic secondborn feelings of being overlooked, unimportant, or out of place in the family.

If an only child is used as an emotional surrogate and is pulled between two warring parents, thirdborn characteristics of mental polarization and mistrust of close relationships may be acted out by the child.

Overprotective parenting which emphasizes the child's "baby" role in the family may lead to youngest-child birth order attributes in an only child.

For several generations, the one-child family has been openly discouraged in many societies, primarily as a security against historically high infant mortality rates and diminished global population as a result of disease, war and natural catastrophes. Human survival in past ages was by no means as "guaranteed" as it appears to be now with modern medicine, sanitation, technology, etc., so large families were probably encouraged simply as a means of ensuring or at least assisting the survival of the species.

Because of this traditional societal attitude, the only child often has a tough reputation to live down. In many cultures, the only-child birth order position is viewed as the wrong approach to reproduction, producing selfish, self-centered, socially maladjusted and overly demanding children. The "baby-boomer" generation which arose in this country after World War II, gave rise to a frenzy of parental concerns about single child families—the one-child family seemed to become even more of a social anathema, and parents' attitudes towards only children were usually characterized by sentiments like: "We just couldn't bear the thought of little Johnny growing up all alone—he'd be so lonely. He'd just never be well socially well-adjusted if he didn't have brothers or sisters to learn to get along with."

Times have changed, and the environmental and over-population concerns of the 1980's and '90's have radically altered the world's outlook on the ideal family structure. Current economic and global issues are now almost dictating one or two-child families. Even China, the world's population giant, has actually outlawed multi-child families.

In America, the psychological traumas experienced by post-war baby-boomers whose parents often had more children than they could economically or emotionally handle, created a new outlook on the efficacy of small versus large family structures, although many American parents still feel that a second child is an indispensable "insurance policy" against the death of an only child.

The identity and self-definition issues involved in the only-child psychology revolve exclusively around the parents. Unlike larger families, in which siblings buffer each other from continual direct parental contacts, the only child has open access to his or her parents, and is usually closely identified with the mother and father's individual characters and their relationship. If the parents are functional, well-defined, self-realized, fulfilled individuals, the only child inherits an excellent and almost incomparable growth opportunity. However, in the case of dysfunctional parents with many unresolved psychological, emotional and identity issues, only children may find it extremely difficult to individuate—to "find" themselves or to separate from their parents' conflicts and problems.

The sense that most only children have of always having the option to go home when the going gets rough in adulthood can be a healthy security valve for functional only children, who feel united yet separate from their parents, but for those from unbalanced family backgrounds, it can serve as an excuse to withdraw from the challenges of living alone and "making it" on their own in the adult world.

Unlike firstborns, only children appear to be more bonded to their mother's, as opposed to their father's psychology. If the mother is lacking in social skills or feels that she does not have a life of her own outside the family, the only child may act out the shyness, lack of self-confidence and weak self-image of the mother. Conversely, if the mother is a strong, take-charge, self-confident individual, the only child will be prone to mirroring these maternal personality strengths.

In the case of a male only child, if the father's role in the family is weak or absent, the male child may step into the father's place, taking on roles and attitudes towards his mother and the family which rightfully belong to the father. In rare cases, this dynamic can lead to mother/son incest, especially if the father is "detestable" or "disgusting" to the mother, and is emotionally or physically absent from the home for long periods of time.

Astrologically speaking, the Moon represents the child's dependence on the mother for survival. Developmentally, the Moon also symbolizes the transition from environmental (family) support to self-reliance—the maturation, or individuation process. Because "leaving the nest", or separating from home and mother, is a particularly difficult issue for only children, the movement and placement of the Moon and its aspects are of special significance in their lives.

For instance, the Moon in aspect to the planet Mars may indicate a period of emphasis on the issue of loyalty to oneself (Mars) as opposed to loyalty to one's mother (Moon). The Mars/Moon balance is always a difficult issue, and in the case of an only child, becomes exaggerated. Dynamic Mars/Moon aspects suggest a difficult transition from the symbiotic mother/child bond to adult independence.

An indication that an only child may have an unresolved Mars/Moon issue could be their feeling that they have no life of their own; that their adult career and relationships are lived more for their mother's gratification than their own. In my practice, I have noted that this "living for my mother" scenario is more often played out by only sons, as opposed to only daughters, because the daughter does not have to support the mother's male gender expectations and pressures: "You're my little man of the family—I know you'll always take care of me".

An only child, whose Moon occupies the sign Scorpio (co-ruler of Mars), the Eighth House or is in aspect to Pluto may be drawn into the influence of Hades or the underworld (Pluto). Within this astrological environment, an only child in a dysfunctional family, may experience an extremely negative mother/child relationship, characterized by resentments, jealously and anger.

The Moon in the sign Scorpio, in the Eighth House or in aspect to Pluto may also suggest that the mother (Moon) has rejected (Pluto) her daughter's gender: "I only had one child—and I really wanted it to be a boy." Because the one-child family is also a tilted family, the same gender issues, (jealousy, competition, etc.), that can come up between two sisters can also occur between a mother and her only-child daughter.

Only-child females are, in fact, far more subject to possible parental gender rejection in that the majority of parents, even today, psychologically need the security of knowing that they are carrying-on the family name and tradition through a male child. Historically, many cultures killed "superfluous" first-born or duplicated female infants and statistically speaking, there are currently almost twice as many male as female only children in the U.S., suggesting that parents will usually try again for a boy if their first child is female.

Female only children often carry subliminal or even conscious feelings of being "worthless" or devalued, because of their parents' unresolved gender disappointment. As adults, these women may correspondingly attract abusive or controlling men in their careers and relationships who reinforce their damaged gender identities. On the other hand, only-child daughters may look for "weak" or effeminate partners on whom they can project their own internal negative feminine image.

In contrast, only-child daughters of parents who welcome and nurture their femininity, tend to develop into very strong, unconventional adult women, who may actually become more independent and confident in life than any other individual birth order position—male or female. Being a loved and nurtured female only-child is an unusual, minority family position in itself, and requires an unconventional attitude on the parent's part, so it's not surprising that this particular birth order position often produces extremely well-differentiated, unconventional women.

The planet Neptune, when connected to the planet Venus, or to the Seventh House, may suggest that the only child has assumed the thirdborn role of mediating, or taking responsibility for conflicts in his or her parents' relationship. Such only children as adults, may feel that they have no right to have satisfying childhood or adult friendships or relationships, because they were unable to fix the problems in their parents' relationship.

The **parents'** birth order, as we have seen, also modifies the way in which all children perceive and play out their birth order roles. In the case of an only child whose parents are both youngest or younger children, the child may be exposed to the parents' younger-child tendency to look to other family members for emotional support and guidance. If **both** parents are younger children, their only child may become the only available family member to fulfill the oldest child, or responsible role in the family.

These types of parents may continually voice their anticipation of the day when their only child will "take care" of them, and the child in this situation can feel the same pressure of family responsibility that an oldest child often carries. However, because there are no younger siblings to care for in this family structure, the only child takes on the role of parent to his or her father and mother.

A situation like this can make life a tremendous ordeal for only children caught in this dynamic. Because of the intense pressure and inappropriate responsibility of this type of role playing, these only children, as adults, may find it difficult or even impossible to perform, even under normal job and relationship pressures and may simply drop out of society altogether.

Only children whose parents were both only children themselves also may face difficult birth order role challenges because, in this dynamic, they tend to psychically attune to and act out every "hole" or unresolved issue in their parents' psychology. This "intergenerational transmission" of unfinished business often occurs to children who duplicate one or more of their parents birth order positions. However, in the situation of the only child with two only-child parents, this "transmission" effect is exaggerated.

On the lighter side of this issue, the combination of an only child and parents who were only children themselves can be one of the happiest and most fulfilling of all birth order combinations if the parents are stable, well-adjusted, fulfilled individuals. In this situation, the only child receives all the benefits of the parents' healthy psychology and the added bonus of the parents empathy and understanding of the special needs and issues of the only-child birth order position.

The only-child male is often heir to the extremely difficult psychology of what Carl Jung termed, the "puer aeternus", or the eternal youth. This syndrome arises, among other reasons, as a result of the close tie between a doting or indulgent mother and her only male child. The mother devotedly cooks, cleans, launders and slaves for her only son and only child, while he is left to indulge his fancies wherever he pleases. His mother encourages and champions her son, without, however, requiring any appropriate developmental responsibilities or requirements of him.

Consequently, the son may never psychologically "come down to earth" because all of the "muck and mire" of "mediocre" existence is all taken care of and left in the capable hands of mother, while he roams free and unhampered, exploring and experimenting with more "significant" other-worldly, poetic or metaphysical concerns. "Puers" may have careers of a highly creative and special nature, however, in many cases, they are unable to solidly commit for any length of time to "mundane" activities—jobs, families, etc. Unfortunately, the high-flying puer many times dramatically "crashes to earth" in a fiery mid-life emotional/psychological crisis, because the obvious signs of physical aging force him to directly confront his own mortality, and the inevitable demise of his "eternal youthfulness".

The placement of a puer's Moon and its aspects often suggest the difficulty that he has in relating to his own feminine, "earthly" anima, or soul. Puers often have their Moon in a Water or an Earth sign, while their Sun, Jupiter and Uranus usually occupy the Air/Fire elements. Any one of these three planets angular suggest a life lived in the "ethers"—separated from mundane and "limited" concrete earthly existence.

But again, astrological symbols in any person's horoscope should always be examined in the context of the person's overall life history. For instance, one of my client's charts indicated an over-abundance of puer elements, and I mistakenly assumed that he was an only child.

However, in discussing his family history I discovered that he had an older brother four years his senior, who had quarreled with the mother and left home at 18, and had never returned or communicated with the family. My client, as the secondborn child, had bonded deeply with his mother, and as he also duplicated his mother's own birth order position, he had been given the family role of his mother's "favorite" son—to the nearly complete exclusion of the elder son who bonded with his "weak" and dominated youngest-brother father.

Because the older brother and his father were, for all intents and purposes, not included in the family "picture" (at least from the dominant mother's perspective), my secondborn client assumed, by default, the position of the only child bonded to the ubiquitous, doting mother, and, consequently, had "imbibed" a large dose of the classic puer psychology. At the time that I saw him, he was embroiled in a critical mid-forties 'crash to earth', and was obsessed by his remorse over never having consistently maintained any long-term career or relationship.

We examined his astrology in the light of his puer psychology, but also in conjunction with his secondborn and youngest birth status which contributed to his lack of identity definition, emotional dependence and failed relationships with women, in which he continually reenacted his favored, overindulged "baby of the family" maternal relationship.

As this example illustrates, probably nothing in astrology is as simple as it seems, and many variables need to taken into consideration when offering astrological counseling.

Another social issue for only children is standing up to people outside the family. Because there are no siblings to do battle with, the only child is often "thin-skinned" and more sensitive than children with siblings, and can be easily offended or pushed around by peers or people in general.

Parents with only children might consider enrolling them in some type of defensive martial art—Aikido, etc., which fosters the psychology of physical and mental self-confidence and strength, so that the child does not continually feel at the mercy of his more "predatory" peers. Participating in a group martial art also assists the child in constructively channeling unexpressed anger and in setting personal boundaries which prevent him from giving or taking on too much for other people.

In that only children often spend a large portion of their developmental years alone, they tend to create their own personal resources or survival skills, such as a strong bond and deep love for books, music, animals or "pet projects". Those who are closely associated with an only child adult or child should understand the time and devotion that they need to "lavish" on these companions or projects, and avoid encroaching on their territory or space.

Only children often become very sociable, affable and friendly adults, enjoying relationships and social interactions outside the home. However, in their romantic relationships, only children, particularly females, can become obsessed by the need to have their partners or mates "all to themselves". Only child adults, just as they can overdo the "togetherness" relationship aspect, can also overdo the socializing aspect, and they benefit most when they balance their social interactions with periods of solitude and reflection which mirror the centering and restful periods of their youth.

The transits and progressions of and to Mars may often cause serious upheavals in the lives of only children. This relates to the issue we discussed—the only child's unexpressed anger at unfamiliar peer abuse which may have been absent in their own single child family. Most children learn to cope with peer conflict by working through fights and disagreements with their siblings. Because the only child has no siblings, their interactions with neighborhood or school children can be new territory, and the peer fights and squabbling they are drawn into can be confusing and frightening. As a result, the only child may feel intense anger without knowing how to cope with or express his or her frustration.

The planet Mars, (brings unexpressed anger to the surface), when aspected by transits from other planets or in its own progressions, represents periods or junctures in the only child's life, when their bottled-up anger may suddenly be triggered or released, sometimes in uncontrollable and destructive ways. High fevers, anemia, skin rashes, eating disorders, adrenal dysfunction or other Mars-related maladies may be indications that the Mars function (aggression, independence) is being suppressed or has not been consciously acknowledged by the only child.

Similar to oldest children, the only child may also develop

hypochondriac tendencies. Being the sole object of the parents' anxieties and concerns, they may internalize these worries and manifest them in the form of environmental allergies, debilitating illnesses, etc. Planets in Virgo or the Sixth House (especially the Moon), or planets in Pisces or the Twelfth House may reflect these dynamics.

If the planet Mars comes into stressful (dynamic) relationship with other planets at the time the ruler of the Sixth or Twelfth House is dynamically aspected as well, sudden, serious and eruptive Mars-related health and psychological issues can come to the forefront of the only child's youthful or adult life. In these cases, astrological counseling that anticipates these critical periods can be the "ounce of prevention" that is worth "a pound of cure."

One only-child scenario that stands out in my mind is that of a 38 year-old single mother of a daughter—"Monique". The interesting thing about this case, in particular, is the variety of family history and birth order influences at work in Monique's life.

Because Monique's father was a firstborn or only child, and her mother was a secondborn, Monique inherited the role of third and lastborn in addition to her only-child birth status. Among other problems, Monique's parents were bitterly polarized over the issue of having more children. Her father was didactically opposed to adding to the family, probably in order to defend his only-child identity as the family's primary recipient of his wife's and daughter's love and attention. On the other hand, Monique's mother felt that her life's purpose could only be fulfilled through having a larger family.

In reviewing Monique's chart, (next page) we see the typical thirdborn "seesaw" pattern, i.e., several of her planets are in direct opposition to each other, and even though her Sun and Moon are not opposing each other by aspect, they occupy the opposing First and Seventh Houses, respectively.

As we already observed in our study of thirdborns in the preceding chapter, many third and lastborns show this polarity "signature" in their charts, which indicates their internal conflicts with opposing issues. In Monique's horoscope, Pluto and Venus

MONIQUE'S CHART

Tropical
Placidus
True Node

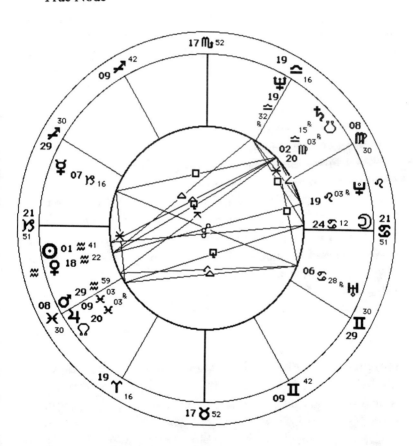

(rulers of the Tenth and Fourth Houses—her parental axis), are exactly opposed each other, indicating her exaggerated or emphasized identification with and assumption of her parents' polarized, confrontational relationship. The core of her chart also suggests Monique's natural desire to create a dialogue between her warring parents.

Although Monique did manifest many thirdborn characteristics in her chart and her behavior, at the same time, she was very much affected by her firstborn and only-child issues—particularly the issues of conformity to parental and societal norms. As an adult, Monique is very much a non-conformist, reflecting, primarily, her female only-child independence—"I'll do it my own way." So, in this sense, her thirdborn referee role was modified by her natural only-child birth order characteristics.

Her First House Mars, Sun and Venus in Aquarius indicate Monique's dominant inclination to be "different", "special" and non-conformist. However, her Capricorn rising, ruler Saturn in the Eighth House, conjunct the south node, point to her possible prior-life patterns (south node) of unconscious "ego-inflation", or an overemphasized assumption of power, which was balanced in this life (north node) by her experience of a sense of powerlessness or vulnerability in her thirdborn mediator role in which she was unable to fix or change her parents conflicted relationship.

Monique may have experienced her thirdborn role in this life in order to balance her prior life tendency towards a "dictator" role (Seventh House Pluto). This might suggest that it is important for Monique to "come down to Earth" (First House planets in Aquarius) in this life and to learn to relate as an equal to "common" people (Aquarius).

Metaphysically speaking, Monique's power issues can be related to her family dynamics in several ways. Her father was a German immigrant, and manifested, in a sense, the "Nietzschean will-to-power", reflected in Monique's Eighth House Saturn (powerful father figure). I would conjecture that Monique chose this particular father figure in order to expose and balance her own past unresolved power issues.

In fact, this has been a notably powerless lifetime for Monique; she has actualized very little of her personal power—she has no primary career, marriage or sphere of influence, either in her social or personal life, through which her character "force" has been expressed.

In Jungian terms, we could say that Monique, at some point in her past, became "identified with the (power) archetype" or universal power source and needs to polarize away from this exaggerated and inappropriate sense of power by experiencing a period of vulnerability which will allow her the freedom to express her "great" self without potential misuses of power.

Monique stated that she had experienced difficulty in supporting herself financially which might relate to her reluctance to conform to the "system". Monique had succeeded in getting a Master's degree in psychology, so I suggested that she consider a position as a child psychologist (Cancer Moon in the Seventh House) or teacher (Jupiter conjoined north node in Pisces). These career choices could be creative and progressive for Monique and would integrate her need for latitude in the workplace, (Uranus in the Sixth House opposing Mercury, ruler of her Sixth House).

Forecasting briefly, I pointed out to Monique that she might be experiencing increasing levels of frustration and anger towards "the establishment", (related to her non-conformity issues and conflicts), during her upcoming Saturn transit to Mars, because the transit would be "asking" her to commit to a more Saturnian, or traditional lifestyle orientation.

Although Saturn often represents an extremely difficult challenge to Moon-oriented only children and thirdborns, I suggested to Monique that since she had assumed both birth order roles, she would benefit by striving for resolution of her nonconformist issues during her Saturn transit and thereby achieve a more balanced and productive lifestyle.

Tips for counseling only children: Suggest the need for balancing polarities such as aggression and passivity, intimacy and personal "space", socializing and introspection, etc. Only-child adults are usually very sensitive people and need sensitive counseling and empathy. Suggest constructive methods of acknowledging and releasing suppressed anger, (Gestalt therapy, rolfing, etc.), and discuss how their aggression or self-assertion can be strengthened through assertive-training therapies, a martial art, etc.

In the case of the "puer" psychology, Jungian psychotherapy or some form of psychodrama or body-related integration therapies can be extremely beneficial.

CONCLUSION

Only children, just as all children in all other birth order positions, need to be seen and treated as individuals. Every child, regardless of his or her astrology or birth order, must be given the opportunity to express the fullness of who they are. In raising our children, I believe that it is imperative for parents to be aware of the enormity of the responsibility that is entailed in providing a family atmosphere that fosters, encourages and supports the delicate, and immensely beautiful process of "unfolding" that occurs in childhood development.

We continually observe this process in nature—caterpillars are transformed into exquisite butterflies, flower buds become beautiful blooms—and no single being or thing is an exact duplicate of another. Why, then, do we as parents, so many times assume that our children can be raised without reference to or acknowledgement of each child's own very specific and special individual preferences and needs?

I think the answer to this may lie in the tremendous complexity that characterizes human development. The enormous number of variables and the survival stresses that humans continually cope with make our growth process an almost infinitely challenging procedure. For this reason, parents must educate themselves in parenting, rather than viewing child-raising as something that just "comes naturally".

If we lived in a completely "natural" environment, this attitude might apply, however, modern society is a far cry from tribal life in which human growth and development largely mirrored the order and elements of the natural environment in which the primitive group functioned. The complex technological age in which we live generates complicated and sometimes seemingly incomprehensible issues and problems. Fortunately, we also have many profound, astute social guides, and professionals who offer enlightened solutions to current complex sociological questions.

Modern-day parents, almost more than anyone else in our

society, need to be aware of current psychological and developmental issues, and today, there are a multitude of parenting books, support groups, seminars and literature that can assist parents in creating nurturing, productive growth environments, so that we, as a society, can move away from producing fragmented, "fractured" adults who, as children suffered sometimes unbelievable, but often unintentional, parental abuse and neglect.

Blending astrology and family psychology is one method among many that can help reveal hidden developmental issues and guide us to more constructive living. Again, I would like to stress, that astrology is best used as a diagnostic tool for revealing important things about our instinctive selves so that we can begin to reconstruct the portions of our identities and psychologies that may have 'strayed off the path' because of improper parental programming.

Treating imbalances in our psyches or personalities should always be left to professional psychologists, counselors and health care practitioners who are skilled in properly channeling and integrating psychological and physical manifestations of unresolved issues and complexes. The astrologer's role is to point out possible existential dynamics, and to refer clients to appropriate professionals for resolution of personal issues.

The art of astrology is, I believe, a tool of great value, and when used in the context of our overall life experiences, can be a truly powerful method for gaining self-awareness. It is my sincere hope that all of us will continue to develop our sensitivity to our inner selves through respectful and enlightened use of this noble ancient art.

My blessings and best wishes to you all.

APPENDIX

The following descriptions of the houses, signs and planets, relate directly to family psychology. These astrological characteristics will, of course, be modified by birth order and other family dynamics. These profiles are not "absolutes", but are meant to be used as starting points in astrological analysis.

THE HOUSES AND SIGNS

The First House/Ascendant and the sign Aries: The initial emergence of identity and of identity formation. The area of the chart indicating the greatest thrust toward individual development and selfhood, which is almost always independent of the direction, attitudes and values of the family. Independence and self-trust versus a perpetual uncertainty and/or fear of the unknown.

The Second House and the sign Taurus: Resourcefulness and "survivability" accomplished by withdrawal from both physical and emotional contact with family members, and from the overall value system of the family, in order to develop one's own values and identity. Integrity and self-reliance versus vicariousness or laziness.

The Third House and the sign Gemini: The understanding and comprehension of explicit forms of communication between all family members which promotes intimacy and mutual respect. Clear, congruent communication and parental instruction versus a schism or split between what is communicated and what is implied.

The Fourth House and the sign Cancer: Family "roots", racial or collective heritage; family or "clan" consciousness. Security and safety versus insecurity and incomplete parent/child bonding, i.e., perceptions that the world is an unsafe, unpredictable place.

The Fifth House and the sign Leo: Self-acknowledgement and validation of one's egocentric needs and creative child-like desires versus an overly needy, self-consumed, insatiable need for affection and attention.

The Sixth House and the sign Virgo: Refers to the competent fulfillment of the "collective" needs of the family as an entire unit through the organized delegation of tasks and duties versus inadequate family management producing "crisis-prone" individuals who feel inherently inadequate and take on the blame for the "flawed" family functioning.

The Seventh House and the sign Libra: Negotiation and communication among family members which allows for free expression of individual values and identity needs within the family group versus little or no cooperation between family members, resulting in limited contact or poor inter-family relationships.

The Eighth House and the sign Scorpio: The destruction of personal limitations through human interchange and relationship. Trust and honesty versus mistrust and manipulation.

The Ninth House and the sign Sagittarius: Respect for each individual's truth, visions, beliefs, and goals within the family versus dogmatic, rigid or blanket generalizations of reality or "truth".

The Tenth House and the sign Capricorn: The rules, laws, and guidelines that are learned within the family which are intended to prepare individuals for entry into society and the world. Consistency and accountability versus hypocrisy and denial.

The Eleventh House and the sign Aquarius: The extension of boundaries and/or values beyond the nuclear family or culture and its norms and taboos. The experience of individuality and uniqueness versus dissociation and "craziness" through inappropriate conformity.

The Twelfth House and the sign Pisces: The teaching of the need for the "highest" form of ethical and moral behavior to all sentient, living things. To be unconditionally loved for being "who you are" in totality, versus playing the role as the family rescuer, scapegoat or martyr.

THE PLANETS

The Sun: The development and objective realization of what one deems as important, life-giving or life-affirming. Secondary narcissism or giving oneself "strokes" without the need for excessive feedback (negative or positive) from others in order to feel important, loved or acknowledged.

The Moon: Imaging and developing a healthy, internal mother figure or guide who provides security, safety and support within a changeable and sometimes unsafe, inhospitable world.

Mercury: The development of clear, consistent communication patterns which assist the growth of individuality and the diversity of each family member. Assists in identifying the difference between what is being said **and** how it is being said. Trusting your "heart's" perception of what is being said versus mental interpretations of family communications.

Venus: Peace of mind and contentment that comes from the healing of discordant or "warring" sub-personalities. Self-love and personal contentment without the NEED (the hole in the soul) for external relationships. Knowing the difference between intimacy and fusion, healthy relationships and entanglements.

Mars: Activities and interests which help to define individuality. Open conflict and the expression of anger and fair fighting are beneficial and constructive. Helps in differentiating between healthy, reasonable risks (emotional and physical) and those that are dangerous or self-destructive or are attempts at trying to "be somebody."

Jupiter: Developing belief systems, morals and rituals which help one to expand into a larger, more comprehensive view of the world on an intuitive and experiential level. Assists in differentiating between what is true for you and what others believe is true. Releasing the need to convert others to your beliefs in order to feel good.

Saturn: The development of internal authority, laws, and morals which are not used as judgments against others. Maturity that allows for taking full responsibility for circumstances and people in your life, rather than blaming them and holding them responsible for the quality of your life experience.

THE "TRANSPERSONAL" PLANETS

Uranus: Developing the capacity to explore confusing, "scary", irrational and movie-like flashbacks that seem to burst upon the "normal" status-quo or reality. You may not be able to differentiate between these mental pictures as images of your past or as portents of your future, but you're open minded and courageous enough to risk the unknown in order to find their origin or meaning.

Neptune: Developing the capacity to extend true compassion and forgiveness to those who have transgressed against you personally or against your highest values, ethics, etc. You may not consciously know the difference between surrendering to your deepest fears or pain, or in other words, authentic suffering vs. self-defeating behavior patterns and inauthentic suffering, but you're truthful enough with yourself to begin this seemingly "endless" task.

Pluto: Developing the capacity to release rage and anger (which poisons your body and soul) towards those who have manipulated, violated or abused you. With all of your will, you're mastering your own internal war and personal conflicts vs. trying to change, transform or control others.

ABOUT THE AUTHOR

Barry D. Cowger has been involved in the field of astrology for more than ten years. He currently has an active astrological counseling practice, and travels extensively, lecturing and conducting seminars on the application of astrology to family dynamics and developmental psychology.

Mr. Cowger is available for personal readings, seminars and lectures. His seminar topics include: **The Impact of Astrology on Childhood Development, Astrology and Parenting, Gender-Typing and Sex Roles in Astrological Analysis, and Horoscopic Interpretations of Birth Order Influences.** These seminars are also available on cassette tapes, which can be ordered directly from the publisher. Please contact Mercurius Publishing, Box 156, Scottsdale AZ 85252, or call 602-949-6007 for scheduling or ordering.

Martha M. Christy is a professional writer, editor and Jungian-oriented counselor. She currently resides in Scottsdale, **Arizona.**

SELECTED WORKS REFERRED TO IN TEXT

PART I
FAMILY DYNAMICS

Chapter One
"I Did It Your Way"

1. Minuchin, S. Families and Family Therapy. Cambridge, MA: Harvard University Press, 1974.
2. Bradshaw, John. The Family, Deerfield Beach: Health Communications, 1988.
3. Hoopes, Margaret H. Birth order and sibling patterns in individual and family therapy. Aspen Publishers, 1987.
4. Perlmutter, M.S. (1984, October) Family myths and birth order. Paper presented at the Annual Meeting Workshop of the American Association of Marriage and Family Therapists, San Francisco.
5. Mindell, Arnold. The Dreambody. Sigo Press, Boston. 1982.
6. Stone, L.A. Birth order and curricular choice. Vocational Guidance Quarterly, 1963, 11(3), pp. 209-211.

Chapter Two
The Parts That People Play

1. Pulakos, Joan. The effects of birth order on percieved family roles. Individual Psychology: Journal of Adlerian Theory, Research and Practice, 1987 (Sep), Vol. 43(3), pp. 319-328.
2. Bradshaw, John. The Family. Deerfield Beach: Health Communications, 1988.
3. Bank, S.P., & Kahn, M.D. The sibling bond. Psychology Today, 1981, (June), pp. 32-47.

Chapter Three
The Circle Game

1. Jung, C.G., Psychological Types, Collected Works, Vol. 6, 1971. Princeton University Press, Princeton, N.J.
2. Perlmutter, M.S., & Wilker, L.M. (1976) Family myths and family types. Unpublished paper. School of Social Work, University of Wisconsin-Madison, Madison, Wisconsin.
3. Beavers, R. Psychotherapy and Growth: A family systems perspective. New York: Brunner/Mazel, 1977.
4. Lewis, J.M.: Beavers, W.E.: Gossett, J.T.; & Phillips, V.A. No single thread: Psychological health in family systems. New York: Brunner/Mazel, 1976.
5. Moy, Samuel & Malony, H. Newton. An empirical study of ministers' children and families. Journal of Psychology & Christianity, 1987 (Spr), Vol. 6(1) pp. 52-64.
6. Pines, Maya. "Superkids," Psychology Today. January, 1979.

PART II
THE BIRTH ORDER PHENOMENON

Chapter Four
Birth Order Rules All

1. Toman, Walter. Never mind your horoscope, birth order rules all. Psychology Today, 1970, (Dec), Vol. 4(7), pp. 45-49, 68-69.
2. Toman, Walter. (1976). Family Constellation (3rd ed.). New York: Springer.
3. Agnthotry, Rekha. Marital adjustment in relation to ordinal birth position. Journal of Psychological Researches, 1986 (Sep), Vol. 30(3), pp. 150-155.
4. Tolan, P.H., & McQuire, D. (1987). Children and family size. In J. Grimes & A. Thomas (Eds.), Children's needs:

Psychological perspectives. New York: National Association of School Psychologists.

5. Freud, S. (1923) The dissolution of the oedipus complex. In J. Strachey, (Ed.), The standard edition of the complete works of Sigmund Freud. London: Hogarth Press, 1961.

6. Adler, A. Characteristics of the first, second and third child. Children, 1928, 3, 14.

7. Zajonc, R.B., Markus, H., Markus, G.B. (1979) The birth order puzzle. Journal of Personality and Social Psychology, 37, pp. 1325-1341.

8. Kidwell, J.S. (1981) Number of siblings, sibling spacing, sex, and birth order: their effects on perceived parent-adolescent relationships. Journal of Marriage and the Family. 43 (May): pp. 50-64.

9. Kidwell, J.S. (1978) Adolescents' perceptions of parental affect: an investigation of only children vs. firstborns and the effect of spacing. Journal of Population 1, pp. 148-166. 10. Kidwell, J.S. The neglected birth order: Middleborns. Journal of Marriage and The Family, 1982, (2) pp. 225-235.

11. Rosenberg, B.G. & Sutton-Smith, B. Sibling age-spacing effects upon cognition. Developmental Psychology, 1969, Vol. 1. No. 6, pp. 661-668.

Chapter Five
Two-Child and "Tilted" Families

1. Forer, Lucille K. Ph.D. Birth Order and Life Roles. Springfield, Illinois: Charles Thomas, 1969.

2. Konig, Karl. Brothers and Sisters. Great Britain: Floris Books, 1958. Reprinted 1984.

3. Galbraith, Richard. Sibling Spacing and Intellectual Development: A Closer Look at the Confluence Models. Developmental Psychology, 18 (March 1982): pp. 151-173.

4. Current Population Reports (1985). Household and Family Characteristics. (Series p-20 No. 371, March).

5. Falconer, Clark W., MD & Ross, Colin A., MD. The tilted

family. Canadian Journal of Psychiatry. Vol. 31. October   1986.

6. Olson, D.H. & Wilson, M. (1985). Family Satisfaction. In D.H. Olson, H.I. McCubbin, H. Barnes, A. Larsen, M.Muxen, & M. Wilson (Eds.) Family Inventories (rev. ed.). St. Paul: Family Social Sciences, University of Minnesota.

7. Cantelon, L.J., Leichner, P.P., & Harper, D.W. (1986). Sex-role conflict in women with eating disorders. International Journal of Eating Disorders, 5, pp. 317-323.

Chapter Six
Large Families

1. Current Population Reports (1985). Household and Family Characteristics. (Series p-20, No. 371, March).

2. Toulitos, J., & Lindholm, B.W. (1980). Birth order, family size and children's mental health. Psychological Reports, 46, pp. 1097-1098.

3. Wadsworth, M. Roots of Delinquency. Oxford: M. Robertson & Co. 1979.

4. Lerner, S., & Schwartz, R. Working systematically with individuals. Paper presented at the Annual Meeting of the American Association for Marriage and Family Therapy, Orlando. Fl. October, 1986.

5. McCubbin, H., & Dahl, B.B. Marriage and family: Individuals and life cycles. New York: John Wiley. 1985.

Chapter Seven
Blended Families

1. Visher, E.B., & Visher, J.S. Stepfamilies: A Guide to Working with Stepparents and Stepchildren. New York: Brunner/Mazel, 1979.

2. Lutz, Patricial. "The Stepfamily: An Adolescent Perspective," Family Relations 32 (July 1983) pp. 367-375.

3. Booth, Alan., & White, Lynn. "The Quality and Stability of

Remarriages: The Role of Stepchildren." American Sociological Review 50 (October 1985): pp. 689-698.

4. Nelson, Margaret., & Nelson, Gordon. "Problems of Equity in the Reconstituted Family: A Social Exchange Analysis," Family Relations 31 (April 1982): pp. 223-231.

5. Craven, Linda. Stepfamilies: New Patterns in Harmony. New York: Julian Messner, 1982.

6. Sauer, Lawrence E. & Fine, Mark A. Parent-child relationships in stepparent families. Journal of Family Psychology, 1988 (Jun), Vol. 1(4), pp. 434-451.

7. Ross, Helgola & Milgram, Joel. "Important Variables in Adult-Sibling Relationships: A Qualitative Study," in Lamb & Sutton-Smith, 1982, Sibling Relationships, pp. 225-249.

8. P. Gebhard, J. Gagnow, W. Pomeroy, & C. Christenson. Sex offenders: An Analysis of Types (New York: Harper and Row, 1965).

9. Finkelhor, D. (1980) Sex among siblings: A survey on prevalence, variety, and effects. Archives of Sexual Behavior, 9, pp. 171-197.

Chapter Eight
Special Families

1. Knapp, Ronald J. When a child dies. Psychology Today, 1987, (Jul), Vol. 21(7), pp. 60-63,66-67.

2. National Center for Health Statistics, US Department of Health and Human Services, Huntsville, Maryland. Statistical Abstracts of the US 105th edition, US Department of Commerce, Bureau of the Census, Washington D.C. 1985.

3. Wasserman, R. (1983). Identifying the counseling needs of the siblings of mentally retarded children. Personnel and Guidance Journal, pp. 622-627.

4. Solnit, Albert J. & Stark, Mary H. (1961). Mourning and the birth of a defective child. Psychoanalytic Study of the Child, 16, pp. 523-537.

5. San Martino, M., & Newman, M.B. (1974). Siblings of retarded

children: A population at risk. Child Psychiatry and Human Development, 4, pp. 168-177.

6. Colangelo, Nicholas. Families of gifted children: The next ten years. Roeper Review, 1988 (Oct), Vol. 11(1), pp. 16-18.

7. McMann, Neal, & Oliver, Ronald. Problems in Families with Gifted Children: Implications for counselors. Journal of Counseling and Development. 1988 (Feb), Vol.(66), pp. 275-278.

PART III
THE MAJOR BIRTH ORDER POSITIONS

Chapter Nine
The Firstborn Child

1. Harris, Irving D., & Howard, Kenneth I. Birth order and responsibility. Journal of Marriage and the Family, 1978, 30, pp. 427-432.

2. Wile, I.S., Davis, Rose: The relation of birth to behavior. Personality in Nature, Society, & Culture. New York, Knopf, 1948.

3. Stone, L.A. Birth order and curricular choice, Vocational Guidance Quarterly 1963, 11 (3), pp. 209-211.

4. Lester, David. Suicide and sibling position. Individual Psychology. Journal of Adlerian Theory, Research, and Practice. 1987 (Sep). Vol. 43 (3) pp. 390-395.

5. Hall, Evelyn G.; Church, Gable E. & Stone, Michael. Relationship of birth order to selected personality characteristics of nationally ranked olympic weight lifters. Perceptual & Motor Skills, 1980 (Dec), Vol 51(3, Pt 1), pp. 971-976.

6. Miller, A. (1984). Thou shalt not be aware. Hildegarde & Hunter.

7. Perls, F.S. Gestalt Therapy Verbatim. Moab, UT, Real People Press, 1969.

Chapter Ten
The Second and Youngest Child

1. Elder, G.H., & Bowerman, C.E. (1963) Family structure and child rearing patterns: The effects of family size and sex composition. American Sociological Review, 28, pp. 891-905.
2. Hoopes, Margaret, H. Birth order and sibling patterns in individual and family therapy. Aspen Publishers, 1987.
3. Kidwell, Jeannie, S. The neglected birth order: middleborn's. Journal of Marriage and the Family, 1982 (2): pp. 225-234.
4. Kennedy, Gregory E. Middleborn's perception of family relationships. Psychological Reports, 1989, 64, pp. 755-760.
5. Kidwell, Jeannie, S. Number of siblings, sibling spacing, sex   and birth order: Their effects on percieved parent-adolescent -

Chapter Eleven
The Third and Middle Child

1. Hoopes, Margaret, H. Birth order and sibling patterns in individual and family therapy. Aspen Publications, 1987.
2. Zimmerman, N., Collins, L., & Bach, J.M., Ordinal Position, Cognitive Style, and Competence: A Systemic approach to supervision. The Clinical Supervisor, Vol. 4(3), Fall 1986, pp. 7-23.
3. Owang, W.N. (1971) Ordinal position, frustration and the expression of aggression. Dissertation Abstracts International 31-B:6243.
4. DeLint, Jan E.E. Alcoholism, birth order and socializing agents. Journal of Abnormal & Social Psychology, 1964, 69 (4), pp. 457-458.
5. Stone, Elizabeth. Ties that bind...and break. Special Report: On Family, May-July 1990.
6. Kurdek, Lawrence A. Siblings' reactions to parental divorce. Special Issue: Children of Divorce: Developmental and clinical issues. Journal of Divorce, 1988-89. Vol. 12(2-3), pp. 203-219.

Chapter Twelve
The Only Child

1. Hawke, Sharryl & Knox, David. One Child By Choice. Office of population research. Princeton University, 1988.
2. Spock, Benjamin. Baby and Child Care. New York: Pocket Books, 1976.
3. Wattenberg, Ben J. The Birth Dearth. New York: Pharos Books, 1987.
4. Freud, A. Normality and pathology in childhood: Assesment of development. In Vol. VI, Writing of Anna Freud. New York: International Universities Press, 1965.
5. Feiring, C. & Lewis, M. Only and firstborn children: difference in social behavior and development. New York: The Guilford Press, 1984.
6. World Press Review. Absentee Fathers. Oct. 1987, p. 59.
7. Time Magazine. Special Issue: Women: the Road Ahead. Fall, 1990.
8. Feldman, Gail. The only child as a separate entity. Psychological Reports, 1978, 42, pp. 107-110.
9. Von Franz, Marie-Louise. Puer Aeternus. Santa Monica, California; Sigo Press, 1981.
10. Hillman, James et al. Puer Papers. Dallas Texas; Spring Publications, 1979.
11. Lewis, Jim. Peter Pan in Midlife. Unpublished manuscript. 1991.

NOTES

NOTES

NOTES

NOTES

To order extra copies of :

RECONSTRUCTING
THE REAL YOU

APPLYING ASTROLOGY
TO
FAMILY PSYCHOLOGY

NAME_____

ADDRESS_____

CITY_____

STATE_____ ZIP_____

	PRICE	QUANTITY	TOTAL
1-4 copies	$12.95 ea.		
5 or more	$10.00 ea.		
		SUBTOTAL	
(For Arizona Residents Only– 6.7%)		TAX	
(1 to 4–$3.00; 5 or more $5.00)		SHIPPING	
		TOTAL ENCLOSED	

☐Check   ☐Amex   ☐VISA   ☐MC   ☐Discover

Acct. # _____ Exp Date_____

Authorized

Signature _____ Date _____

MAKE CHECKS PAYABLE TO:

Mercurius Publishing
Box 156
Scottsdale, Arizona 85252
602-949-6007 * Fax 602-991-8387

☐ PLEASE SEND ME INFORMATION ON
BARRY COWGER'S SEMINARS AND LECTURES!

To order extra copies of :

RECONSTRUCTING
THE REAL YOU

APPLYING ASTROLOGY
TO
FAMILY PSYCHOLOGY

NAME_____

ADDRESS_____

CITY_____

STATE_____ ZIP_____

	PRICE	QUANTITY	TOTAL
1-4 copies	$12.95 ea.		
5 or more	$10.00 ea.		
		SUBTOTAL	
(For Arizona Residents Only– 6.7%) TAX			
(1 to 4–$3.00; 5 or more $5.00) SHIPPING			
		TOTAL ENCLOSED	

☐Check   ☐Amex   ☐VISA   ☐MC   ☐Discover
Acct. # _____ Exp Date_____
Authorized
Signature _____ Date _____

MAKE CHECKS PAYABLE TO:

Mercurius Publishing
Box 156
Scottsdale, Arizona 85252
602-949-6007 * Fax 602-991-8387

☐ PLEASE SEND ME INFORMATION ON
BARRY COWGER'S SEMINARS AND LECTURES!